RULES OF THE GAME

How to Achieve Good Success Without Selling Your Soul

SUSAN GORDON KINNANE

RULES OF THE GAME. Copyright © 2024. Susan Gordon Kinnane. All Rights Reserved.

Printed in the United States of America.

No portion of this book may be reproduced, stored in a retrieval system, or transmitted in any form or by any means, except for brief quotations in printed reviews, without the prior written permission of DayeLight Publishers or Susan Gordon Kinnane.

ISBN: 978-1-958443-76-7 (paperback)

DEDICATION

This book is dedicated to my beloved children, Monique and Malik; my grandson, Micah Lee; my mother, Delores; and my siblings, Sandra, Kirk and Latoya.

It is also specially dedicated to the memories of my deceased and eldest sister, Dawn; my nephew, Raheim; my grandfather, George Gordon; my grandmother, Rhoda; my father, Trevor Gordon; my aunt, Daphne; my beloved mentor, Dr. Chloe Morris; and my dear friend, Claudia.

To my prayer partners and the Deborah N.O.W. Ministry partners, your support has been the wind beneath my wings.

Special dedication as well to Meloney "Pam" Lewis whose invitation to the courts of the Lord changed the trajectory of my life and to Rev. Rohan Ambersley who preached the message of salvation that led me to Christ.

This book was birthed and produced because of your impact in my life and I am forever grateful. I therefore dedicate it to you.

ACKNOWLEDGEMENTS

It was in 2005 at a fasting service that Bishop Stevenson Samuels exclaimed, "You really should write a book!" It was much later in July 2014 that I wrote the first line for this book, but Pastor Sam, as he is affectionately called, activated the seed in me to share my miraculous journey. For over fifteen years, he served as my pastor and witnessed the different seasons of my life; he also became my coach. I could not have asked for a more experienced servant leader to guide me as he had navigated both the secular and spiritual spaces of life, serving in many capacities from the trenches to the boardroom. I am forever grateful for his warmth and willingness to listen to my out of the box thoughts and visions.

Patrick Kinnane watered the seed the seed for this book as we travelled for twenty-three hours from Jamaica to Australia during our first trip. A far contrast from the valleys of Hermitage surrounded by green mountains, it resonated in me in that moment in Australia that my life's journey is nothing short of a miracle. It dawned on me that I did beat the odds and should tell the story. Many thanks are therefore due to both of these gentlemen: to Patrick for watering my soft side at home and ensuring that I had a balanced life, and to Pastor Sam for igniting my tenacity and "fanning into flame" my gift for serving in ministry. With their guidance, I was a force to be reckoned with in the marketplace as I knew I had "backative." Each experience has allowed me to compile notes for this book.

This book emanates from over thirty-five years of personal observation, studying the lives of successful servant leaders and I thank them all for blazing the trail for us to follow.

A deep sense of gratitude firstly to *Veronica Stone* who encouraged me to purchase my first home at age 31 and to *Bridget Brown* for being a destiny helper in the process. This investment positioned me to be successful in other areas of my life and I am forever grateful.

Heartfelt gratitude as well the following people who have impacted me significantly and are the architects behind this writing:

- *Yvonne Clarke-Facey* (now deceased), my basic school teacher and one of the best teachers in early childhood education. Your care and diligence in the classroom opened my desire to serve and to be lifelong learner.
- *Hugh Ingram*, my high school mathematics teacher. Thanks for sparking my confidence with numbers and for being a bridge for me to serve my alma mater, Excelsior High School.
- Wendy McLean (deceased), my first counsellor in the Social Work profession. I am forever grateful for

your emphasis on counselling and growth to self-knowledge. Thanks also for your encouragement to pursue my passion in sales.
- Ama Ababio, a spiritual midwife who inspired me to excel in my tertiary education pursuits. Thank you for all you do to enrich the lives of others.
- *Amy DaCosta*, my first supervisor. Thank you, Mrs. D. for ensuring that we worked hard unapologetically. Your confidence, courage and kindness have shaped my approach to leadership and inspired me to go above and beyond in answering the call of duty.
- *Donovan McCalla*, the man who showed me the importance of dressing for success, leading by example and keeping myself accountable. Thank you for your contribution to my development.
- *Marva Johnson*, for being the bridge as I entered the corporate space. I will forever cherish your invaluable guidance.
- *Egbert Chang* (now deceased), recruiting manager in the heaving equipment industry. I am grateful for your humility, patience and unimpeachable loyalty.
- *Fuzz Lechler*, thank you for being authentic, steadfast in the game and compassionate to all.
- *Angella Scott-Brown*, thank you for showing me what guts, loyalty and trust look like.
- *Sergio Soto*, your ability to negotiate and command a room are enviable. You are a confident and

inspirational leader whose words of "I believe in you" have made a huge difference in my life
- *Jose Sasso*, a firm yet compassionate leader. You taught me not to "be a kiss up" or feign affections. Instead, I should let my words speak for me. I am grateful for your advice.
- *Jaco Nolte*, my mentor. You have shown me the possibility of consistency and professionalism from day one. I thank you for not only supporting my journey in the corporate world, but for also believing and supporting my charity aspirations through Deborah N.O.W. Ministry.
- *Angel Gomez*, your authenticity and love for humanity are unmatched. Your brilliance in leading us was only matched by your candid way of connecting with all. I am forever grateful for the opportunity to learn from you.
- *Andres F. Cuadros and Carlos Magalhaes*, you were two constants through the most difficult time in my career. Your presence was like anchor for my soul. Thank you!
- *Alwein, Asif, Freek and Nigel*, my learning and travelling partners. You are cherished friends and I thank you being my cheerleaders.
- *Roy Howell*, a man for all seasons and a leader in the field of play in heavy equipment. You identified my gift and served as my confidant and friend. Thank you for your class and dedication and for being the epitome of a family man.

- *Patrick Goulbourne*, a man with unmatched integrity who mentored me and taught me so much about management. Thank you so much.
- *Magion Stephenson*, you rescued me from the consequences of a desperate financial mistake and taught me to "count the cost before I mount the horse." Thanks for being a friend indeed.
- *Howard Stewart*, the man who took me under his wings. You are a pioneer in your field. Your time and guidance helped me navigate the arduous paths in the game and I am grateful.
- *Hanna Stella,* many thanks for your kindness during my overseas work assignment.
- *Tamara Thompson*, thank you for being a consummate servant leader who continues to compassionately lead and be a partner in ministry.
- *Michelle Hinds-Dennis*, I am grateful for your financial counsel, accountability and support.
- *Angella Wander*, thanks for your encouragement and helpful feedback of my presentations and other initiatives.
- *Robert Williams*, you kept my career alive through your patronage as you brilliantly led in the heavy equipment industry. I am so thankful for you.
- *Tashaleen Morgan the best in the field of mortgage cconsultants and lifelong friend*

Antoon Karg & Sharon Marteens for being an advocate and supporter during one of life's greatest challenge

I am also indelibly grateful to the following persons who have been a steady source of spiritual support:

- My pastor, *Bishop Leslie Pinnock*. Your prayers, spiritual counsel and support have kept me even in some of the darkest moments of my life.
- Lorene Pinnock ministry partner and loyal supporter in business.
- My former pastor, *Bishop Cornel Shaw*. Thank you for your consistent spiritual counsel and for being a safe space and support for my children, especially Malik. Thanks for your compassion and care during the toughest times of my life.
- *Bishop Dr. Rohan Ambersley* for sharing the salvation story as I surrendered my life to Jesus Christ. Thank you for being my professional coach and friend.
- *Bishop Paul Morris and Rev Sandra Morris*, thank you for being my constants and confidants.
- *Bishop Horace and Benita Aiken*, thanks for being the conduits of miraculous moments and support.
- *Delfose "Junior" McDermott and Valrie "Rosie" Neil*, I will always cherish your unconditional love, support and encouragement.
- *Dr. Chloe Morris* (deceased), my mentor and dear friend. Your life's mission was to lead a prayerful life. You taught me the importance of seeing purpose in all that life has to offer. I am grateful for your tutelage and many lessons to be present and

productive, and to live a life of honour in all aspects of my life.
- *My prayer partners*: Angela Smart, Prophetess Charmaine Wood, Dr. Felicia Grey, Denise Curtis, Rev. Georgia Haffenden and Dr. Sophia Gabriel. For over sixteen years, you have been a source of accountability, vulnerability, dedication and support. Thank you for holding me, my family and plans in your prayers always.
- *The Deborah N.O.W. Executive members*: Bishop Paul Morris, Rev. Sandra Morris, Benita Aiken, Dr. Felicia Grey, Rev. Georgia Haffenden, Jacqueline Powell, Colleen Cohen and Sabrina Bryce along with our cadre of esteemed youth volunteers; *Dr. Alicia Louis-Potter and Empowered Women International*, corporate sponsors, conference speakers, and partners - thank you for sharing in the vision for the last twelve years
- *Escarpment Road New Testament Church of God congregants*, many thanks for entrusting me to serve as a Deaconess since 2013. To my colleagues on the board, we share lifelong bonds as we committed our time in service. We have been in the valley of the shadow of death and have shared many glorious moments. Thank you for being a central part of my life.
- *Cerise Casserly*, my cousins and sister in ministry. I am thankful for your support, wise counsel and love.

- *Alvia Bonfield-Johnson,* I am grateful for your consistent support in both ministry and the corporate world.
- *Grace Benda – prayer partner, confidant and friend. Thank you.*
- *Melisa Daley & Peter Arscott your friendship, love and support have made life an absolute joy.*
- *Mrs Allison Peart your love for humanity, serving others and your Excelsior High School family have been an inspiration. Thank you.*
- *Tricia Roberts and Lorraine Cousins,* many thanks for being dedicated sponsors of Deborah N.O.W. Ministry initiatives.

Special thanks as well to my friends and family members who have enriched my life in tremendous ways:

- *Michelle and Rosemarie Thompson,* thank you for making friendship a joy.
- *Jacqueline Powell,* you are a friend for a lifetime and I am grateful for your unfailing love and support.
- *Jayson Downer supporter in ministry and friend - Thank you*
  Sophia Grant, Jacqueline Henry and Gregory Wiggan, my high school friends who are now family. Many thanks for your years of friendship.
- *Ryan Dawes,* thanks for your care, dedication, loyalty and inspirational support.

- *Ryan Blackwood*, a mentor for my son who invited us into the world of chess. We are very grateful for the life skills that you imparted and your support over the years.
- *Philippot Brown*, my son's football coach. Thank you for being a strong source of support during his high school years.
- *Jimmy Sylvester*, an international student who served as an educational travel companion. You came at just the right time in my life's journey. I will always cherish your contribution to my life.
- *Terri Creary, Jacqueline James and Sharon Knibbs*, your friendship and encouragement are unmatched.
- *Annmarie Murray*, words cannot express my love and appreciation for you.
- *Anette Campbell and Joylene Miller*, thanks for your faithfulness, trust and support.
- *Heather Davis*, thank you for taking the time to read my thoughts and write the foreword. Thanks for your years of friendship.
- *Dr. Felicia Grey*, thanks for reading the manuscript and giving me valuable feedback. I am so grateful for your insight, counsel and friendship.
- *My mother*, Delores Leslie; *sibling*s Burchell, Sandra and Latoya, thank you for your unfailing support during my trials in life and for being a safe place to be myself.
- *My children Monique and Malik* and my *grandson, Micah Lee*, thanks for making parenting a joy.

To my editor *Crystal Daye* and Dayelight Publishers, this book would not have materialized without you. Many thanks for your patience and high level of professionalism.

To my executive administrative assistants throughout the years, *Farrah Robotham and Maranda Suckoo*; thank you for your dedication and attention to detail. Your commitment to the task has enriched the work environment and I am grateful.

Dr. Wayne Henry, a brother and mentor in Christ. Thank you for answering the call and for your wise counsel even in challenging times.

Finally, all glory and praise my Lord and Saviour, Jesus Christ. In Him I move, serve and have my being.

My heart is filled with gratitude to see this project come to life and I thank you all for being a part of the journey.

TABLE OF CONTENTS

Dedication iii

Acknowledgements v

Foreword 17

Preface 19

Introduction 23

The First Half: Start! 29

Chapter 1: Players in the Game 35

Chapter 2: Finding Common Ground 51

Chapter 3: Giver or Taker? 67

Chapter 4: Connecting 83

The Second Half: Shift! 95

Chapter 5: Values 101

Chapter 6: Share the Vision 109

Chapter 7: Restoration 127

Chapter 8: Win: The Peak 141

Bibliography 161

About the Author 165

FOREWORD

Susan and I met in 2004 when she surrendered her life to Christ. It is hard to be a stranger to her because her friendly and outgoing personality makes it easy to connect with her. She is a real individual. Her life is a living example of someone who lives daily not focussing on the negatives but seeing and seizing the opportunities and taking advantage of them. She is a natural role model for those who would push through the challenges of a humble beginning, dared to think and dream big, and watch with patience, commitment and hard work as the dream becomes a reality.

She never misses an opportunity to be a blessing to others, even if that sometimes means putting the needs of others ahead of her own. This speaks well of her taking heed to the Scripture to not think of herself more highly than she ought to, but in humility consider others better than herself (Philippians 2 v 3). She is a woman of substance, class and most importantly, she is genuine.

Antoinette (as she is affectionately called) has a mind for business and that is abundantly clear from a first conversation with her. As you read her story, you will see the genesis of the seed that was planted in her and how it was watered and nurtured to become the fruit that is evident and beneficial for so many today. Susan's desire for the success of others, especially her family members is unparalleled. The challenge and encouragement she shares in the book are a testimony of the value she places on sharing information with others to help them succeed.

The book you are reading is the answer to years of prayer and commitment as our prayer group met every Saturday night to pray, asking The Lord for wisdom and direction, insight and favour and every good success for every leg of the journey to where it is now in your hand or on your device. It is an answered prayer.

It is an honour to have been a part of this journey and I am confident that what you will read in this her first book, will challenge and encourage you to achieve good success without selling your soul.

Well done, Sister. We look forward to the next book.

Heather A. Davis

PREFACE

"What does it mean to sell your soul, Ms. G?" This was the question that my young supervisee asked me one day as we sat together in the office. He seemed very perturbed and wanted a real answer. We live in a world where many people who reach the pinnacle of success are believed to have done so by "selling their souls", so I explained to him what the concept means.

I told him that it means to go against the core of what one believes and do something that is against God's plan for one's life just to be successful. As a believer in Christ, I also quoted Psalm 20 v 7:

"Some trust in chariots, and some in horses;
But we will remember the name of the Lord our God"
(NKJV).

I used this to suggest to him that our confidence should be in God and not in other things that may entice us to get the job done quicker but in immoral ways. I am not sure what decision he was wrestling with, but this answer satisfied him – and this is how this book was born.

Rules of the Game: How to Achieve Good Success Without Selling your Soul is my story. I am a sports enthusiast and love watching a good game of football. I also enjoy track and field and have spent many days in the Jamaican national stadium cheering on the athletes, jumping for joy when one of my favourites wins a race or shouting out "GOAL!" when the team scores. I have also left some of these games disappointed in the outcome and frustrated with some of the match officials' decisions. There are many lessons that we can learn from athletes who endure the rigours of training, often sacrificing and delaying gratification to achieve success. These lessons are especially striking in those who not only participate in individual events, but in team sports as well. Far more is required when players realize that whatever they do impacts not just their future, but that of the team as well.

Life is set up just like these games. We do some things on our own, but there are others where our decisions have consequences for our family members, friends and work colleagues. In other words, like the athletes at the games, we are all doing life based on a given set of rules. Sometimes we are fouled, impeded in the lane that we are running, or the other team unexpectedly gets a penalty. Other times we are side-lined on the bench or ejected from the game with a red card. Despite these outcomes, however, we pull on the support coming from the people in the arena of our lives, get back in the game and overtime, return to our winning ways.

Using the analogy of life as a game with its own rules, this book therefore encourages readers to pursue their goals while remaining true to their core values. It also emphasizes the fact that it is possible to find joy and contentment in every area and stage of life. As you read this book, you will find that it not only highlights the call to be cognizant of one's moral compass, but hopes to stir in you the reader, a conviction of service to mankind with courage, compassion and consistency. I invite you on this journey as I narrate the story of my life from the valleys of my hometown, to the major leagues of the corporate world where I often sit as the only female at the table. My experiences required me to find the grace, grit and gumption to overcome the many tackles, fouls, red cards and unexpected penalties of life to score victories even in improbable circumstances.

Using the wisdom collected from the years of working in different sectors as a sales professional, licensed social worker, kingdom builder and philanthropist, I candidly share how the trajectory of my life and interactions with people from all walks of life have helped me to create a winning attitude without selling my soul. It is my wish that you will find this story meaningful, and that you will adopt some of these strategies as you aim to succeed in the Game of Life.
Read this book to learn the rules of the game and the penalties to avoid. Read this book if you want to win but stay true to your authentic self. Read this book if you are ready

to start the journey towards success. As you read, may your life be fuelled by possibilities, powered by passion and sustained by purpose. May these anecdotes and analogies provide you with instructions on how to gauge your desires, measure your decisions and be deliberate about your destiny. May this story inspire you to win and to win without selling your soul. Are you ready? Let's Go! Ready. Set. Go. Game on!

Susan Gordon Kinnane

INTRODUCTION

All across the world, people engage in different types of games. Some of these are played for the sheer fun of it, while others are played competitively and for profit. The Olympic Games, held every four years, is a global event that showcases the best of the world's sports teams and individual players as they compete for the glory of their country, their families and friends. The first Olympic Games were held in 776 BC in Olympia Greece, and were a part of a religious festival held to honour the Greek god, Zeus. The first set of games featured only men and winners were given a wreath of leaves as the symbol of victory. By 393 AD, the Games were banned by Emperor Theodosius I and remained so for many years. It was later in 1894 that the Frenchman Baron Pierre de Coubertin revived what has become known as the Modern Olympics (Penn Museum, 2023; Sakavitsi, 2024). The International Olympic Committee (IOC) was also created at that time and an Olympic motto proposed. This motto - *Citius, Altius, Fortius*, is the Latin for *"Faster, Higher, Stronger"* and describes the types of sports that are involved in the Games. On July 20, 2021, the IOC made an amendment to the Olympic motto. It now reads, *"Citius, Altius, Fortius – Communiter"*. It means, *"Faster, Higher, Stronger – Together"*, with "together" added to signify the unifying

23

nature of sport and the importance of that unity across the world. We therefore go faster, higher and stronger, together (IOC, 2024).

The IOC recognizes four main different types of sports. These include individual, partner, team and extreme sports. Archery and boxing are examples of individual sports, while figure skating and badminton would fall under partner sports. Examples of team sports include American football and lacrosse, while base jumping, ice climbing and paragliding are types of extreme sports (Leadership and Sport, 2021). All of these sports are governed by a set of rules that both constitute and regulate each game. This means that the rules are what create the game in the first place and are also used to keep players in check. The rules, for example, would determine how many players can be used in the game (constitutive rule) and then used to govern the game so that this rule is not violated (regulative rule). A rule is therefore "an accepted principle or instruction that states the way things are or should be done, and tells you what you are allowed or are not allowed to do" (Cambridge Dictionary).

Every game has its own rules. In soccer (known as football in some parts of the world), for instance, the game is played with two teams, with seven players needed from each side to start the game. One of these players must be the goalkeeper. This game has a "no hands" rule, with only the goalkeepers allowed to use their hands. Other players have to use body parts such as their feet, head and chest to move the ball. If these players touch the ball, it is called a handball and a foul and can result in a penalty for the opposing team. The penalty is given at the referee's discretion, and is taken 12 yards from the middle of the goal line. The referee manages the game and can issue a yellow card to caution a player. If the player accumulates two yellow cards in the same game, this converts to a red card and the player must leave the field. The referee may also issue a red card to a player who commits a serious offense. This player must leave the field and cannot be replaced for the rest of that game (The Basic Rules of Soccer).

The rules that govern basketball differ from those that regulate soccer. Basketball is also played with two teams, but only five players from each team can be on the court at any one time. Each team aims to shoot more field goals (goals scored during play) than the other, with field goals worth two or three points depending on where the shot is taken from. These goals can take the form of "jump shots, layups, slam dunks, and tip-ins" (Basketball Rules Explained). The National Basketball Association (NBA) allows each team five fouls per quarter, which can range from personal, flagrant, offensive and technical, depending on their level of severity and their violation of the administrative, possession and personal contact rules. Teams use these guidelines along with other regulations around time, defense and offense to maximize their efforts to win the game (Basketball Rules Explained).

This book uses the parallel of life as a game to underscore the fact that regardless of where we live, work and spend our time, there are rules that govern every activity that we participate in. In the same way that games are played learning both the constitutive and regulative rules, so must we learn and play the rules of life. Many athletes in their quest to reach the zenith of success, take short cuts by using illicit drugs, misrepresenting their age, or avoiding drug tests. These short cuts, however, often lead to disgrace as the athlete's cheating is usually discovered, leading to punitive responses such as bans, retractions of the medals won and a stain on their career. Sadly, if the athlete cheated while being a member of a team, the other team members also suffer as they also lose the medals that they would have won with that athlete. This book likens the cheating athlete to the many ways that we compromise our values in order to get that promotion, accolade or other form of advancement on the job or in our other areas of endeavour. It calls this cheating, "selling your soul."

Rules of the Game: How to Achieve Good Success Without Selling Your Soul encourages the reader that it is possible to be successful without compromising one's values. Consistent with the game metaphor, Section One is dubbed, "The First Half" and has a "Quarter Break." It includes several game rules and coaching tips that serve as guidelines for how to start, be authentic, connect with others and pay it forward. Section Two is "The Second Half". Life sometimes takes us into unforeseen territory and this will require us to shift our perspective. "The Second Half" therefore exhorts us to share the vision, keep the scores, shoot on target and win. The book closes with some thoughts on "Game Over" and how we can prepare ourselves for the final whistle when we exit the game of life. This book takes you on a journey with the author where you will silently sigh, cheer and maybe even cry as you travel on the highs and lows of this riveting story. You will be challenged, motivated and inspired to learn from your defeats, but to remain undefeated in the game of life. Most of all, you will be encouraged to actively pursue your dreams, fully confident that it is possible to achieve success without selling your soul.

Felicia A. Grey, Ph.D.

THE FIRST HALF

START!

"Start by doing what is necessary: then do what's possible and suddenly you are doing the impossible."
Saint Francis of Assisi

The countries travelled, experiences gained and life-long relationships that I have had are a far contrast from the valleys of my hometown. In this community, the bell on the campus of the University of the West Indies' which we called "The Cauchy" was our alarm clock. The University of the West Indies, Mona Campus sits on two former sugar plantations and the alarm bell still dongs to this day. If the "Cauchy" caught you at home or the bus stop, you knew you would be late for school or work. This "Cauchy" continued to regulate our activities during the evenings because when we as children heard it, we knew it was time to ensure that the yard was swept and all dishes were clean.

An understanding of sticking to a routine and doing the necessary things was forged early and this fostered discipline in my formative years. I can still hear the shouts of Ms. Thelma calling my brother and me as she accompanied us to the bus stop so as to avoid the rush to get a space on it. This was usually before the break of daylight and we needed to walk a quarter mile to catch the bus to avoid the crowd when the bus entered our community. Ms Thelma is one of my early examples of a hardworking entrepreneur who cared deeply about others. In many ways, what she achieved can be deemed as the impossible as she worked assiduously with what she had, making her business a success.

Ms. Thelma was a resident fruit vendor who sold her fruits at the entrance of the community and the bus usually passed there before it got to the terminus. She peddled her wares of fresh bananas and oranges in her enamel pan. Her consistent action of selling fresh fruits provided breakfast to many of us and was the easiest and most accessible nutritional meal for some of us. Ms. Thelma's dedication in guiding us, a group of children of ages ranging from six to twelve years old safely to the bus stop, demonstrated her diligence and care and ensured that we had a good start.

A good start meant getting to school on time and having a meal to begin our days. This cements the truth of Saint Francis of Assisi's quote - "Start by doing what is necessary." We understood our assignment in that era of our lives and Ms. Thelma facilitated our start in the game. All of us who walked together with her as children are now lifelong friends. There is a warmth and fire that is rekindled when we meet at events to reminisce on those days. There is also a confidence among us that only we who experienced those early morning walks hand-in-hand with Ms. Thelma can identify with.

Today, Ms. Thelma is no longer with us, but her memory is forever etched in the minds of the children of the 1980s in Hermitage for the start she gave us. Back then, we did not fully grasp the magnitude of her impact and would facetiously call her "Ms. Tell Ma" behind her back. She would lovingly correct us and if needs be, spoke with a drawl to warn us, "I'm going to tell you ma!" All of us for most part of the 1980s era who benefited from this experience of "It takes a village to raise a child" have done well and are now productive members of the global village. We are also cognizant of the fact it is possible to be anything one desires to be. All we have to do is just start.

Today, every step, every table, and every game that I am involved in, I recognize that I stand on the shoulders of those who have gone ahead of me. Because of their impact, I have the discipline and diligence to win in the game of life. Where I am today is as a result of this start by a village mother who showed me and others compassion and consistency. These characteristics are ones that you can emulate as you also start in any area of your life.

Coaching Tip #1: Think back on your life and try to identify someone who helped you to be where you are today. Many of us have a village mother, school teacher, pastor, community leader or other mentor who spoke life into us when we were younger. For us, it was Ms. Thelma. You will have another name, but the role they played is similar. How did that person's commitment to doing the seemingly mundane and "small" but necessary tasks help to give you a good start? How did that start help you to do the possible and then propel you into the impossible? As you identify them, write a note of gratitude and commit to giving at least one other person a "good start" in life.

My Good Start in Life Gratitude Note

As I reflect on my life's journey, I am thankful to

_____

_____

_____

Rules of the Game

_____

_____
who helped me in my early years.

Because of his/her/their impact, today I am able to

_____

_____

_____

_____

_____

_____

I commit to helping at least one other person get a good start in life.

CHAPTER 1

PLAYERS IN THE GAME

"Service of the whole humanity is the duty of everyman."
Mahatma Gandhi

All of us are linked in the game of life. Our families, jobs and communities may place us in different "divisions", but essentially, we are all a part of the same team. This commonality is what binds us as humans and makes it important for us to lead lives of service that benefit humanity. Every act of kindness therefore forms an arch as it flows from us to others and back to us in multiplied ways. All of us are players and we all have a role to play.

Recognizing the importance of service to humanity, my philosophy is that love, mindfulness, and ethical behaviour are fundamentals in living a fulfilled life. Like Gandhi, I give by serving all of humanity and living by the Golden Rule of doing unto others as I would have them do unto me (Matthew 7: 12). These two powerful concepts underscore the value of empathy and compassion in our interactions with others. Living a life marked by love involves being mindful of fellow humans and all living beings and recognizing the interconnectedness of life.

Authenticity, ethical and moral behaviour shape our roles in society. Upholding self-respect, tenacity, and hard work while honouring the Creator through our actions are noble aspirations that contribute positively to the human experience. Like Paul in Romans 8, we see virtues such as dignity, bravery, and passion, and holding these qualities will inspire us on our journey toward fulfilling our destinies and serving others. It is a beautiful synthesis of philosophical and spiritual ideas that encourage us to lead lives filled with compassion, integrity, purpose, and realness. Understanding who we are in God can also help us to serve boldly as our most authentic selves. The verses below capture this well:

"This resurrection life you received from God is not a timid, grave-tending life. It's adventurously expectant, greeting God with a childlike "What's next, Papa?" God's Spirit touches our spirits and confirms who we really are. We know who he is, and we know who we are: Father and children. And we know we are going to get what's coming to us—an unbelievable inheritance! We go through exactly what Christ goes through. If we go through the hard times with him, then we're certainly going to go through the good times with him!"
(Romans 8:15-17, The Message)

Authenticity

Hope, faith, and contribution are intrinsic to the human experience. Hope provides the motivation to persevere through challenges, faith offers strength in times of uncertainty, and contribution gives our lives meaning and purpose. These, coupled with belief in oneself help you to remain authentic and are critical for good success without losing your soul.

Self-belief provides the foundation for pursuing goals, overcoming obstacles, and realizing one's potential. It is important to note, however, that success should not come at the expense of one's values or moral compass. Maintaining integrity and staying true to yourself, even in the face of challenges or temptations, are essential for long-term fulfilment and inner peace.

Success that is built on a strong sense of self and guided by ethical principles is not only more sustainable, but also more meaningful. It allows individuals to achieve their goals while remaining grounded in their values and preserving their integrity and authenticity.

Authenticity plays a crucial role on this journey. Living authentically means being true to yourself, aligning actions with values, and embracing vulnerability. It allows us to connect more deeply with others and contribute to the world in a genuine way.

By nurturing hope, strengthening faith, and embracing authenticity, individuals can contribute meaningfully to the advancement of their communities and the world at large. It is a powerful combination that fosters personal growth and positive change. Anyone who strives to win in life should therefore do so authentically.

In defining my game and having thirty-one years in the corporate world working primarily in sales, I got a first-hand view of how the game is played. During this time, I also discovered my strengths, weaknesses, and everything in between. Every team has one goal, albeit coaches, referees, and spectators have varying desires or missions in each moment of play. To win, one must understand the guidelines that govern the sport that they play. In netball, one must pivot and play, whilst in football, one dribbles and play. It is equally important to know your role in the team to win. Each player has a different role and it is only by conforming to the rules of that role can the overall team do well. Defenders must therefore defend, forwards aim for the goal and goal keepers protect the net. Winning therefore requires a plan, a clear process, and an end game. **Authenticity on and off the field will help to determine the game** as teammates will come to trust you and be confident that you are committed to the plan.

Game Rule #1:
To win, one must understand the guidelines that govern the sport that they play.

My Father, My First Coach

My father was my first business coach. He had a game plan that I would be the star in the arenas of business by age fourteen. Under his tutelage, I therefore became a seasoned manager of my family's establishment. I had been doing the books since the age of twelve. My father believed in my mathematical abilities and would never pass an opportunity to encourage me by declaring at every opportunity that I was a star.

Words of affirmation flowed freely in my home. My father spoke prophetically over my life and destiny. He would say things to me like - *"You are so much like my mother. Just as Mary Gordon lit up the town square with her fancy dresses, you will light up the world with your wit, willing spirit, and wanderlust nature."* I received and believed every word. A wall chart with the poem, Desiderata by Max Ehrmann adorned our home and its words resonated me. I believed with all my heart that I am "a child of the universe no less than the trees and the stars; I have a right to be here." These words have stayed me and now as a mother, **I am determined for my children to recognise and believe that they have a right to life and a place at the table**.

My father and I loved traveling, and as we travelled, we would have many heart-to-heart and also light-hearted conversations. Our conversations included the importance of education, and the criticality of being honourable in all business transactions, politics, sex, sports, religion, and race.

Daddy would make every effort to attend parties or dances that contracted his sound system and supported the "bar" as he would call it. He was also a practical teacher. One night, while passing a vacant lot after we finished one of his gigs as sound system owner, we saw cars going to and from the dark lot. He sighed, then uttered, *"Only fifty dollars! Women are prostituting themselves over that lot for as little as fifty dollars because they do not recognise their value."* He then said to me, "Know and remember this, my daughter. Get an education and you will be able to pick, choose and refuse." Daddy always left a word or two off his sentences, but I got the message very clearly. I felt, in that moment, that he was impressing upon me the value of a good education, respect for my bodily autonomy, and how an education can be the avenue through which I make responsible life choices. I heard him loudly and clearly and took very seriously my responsibility to get educated, and then to in turn educate, empower and enrich lives.

My self-confidence was concretized as he went on to say, *"Know your worth; it is immeasurable. Never put a dollar value to your worth – no money can buy your worth. Never owe anyone cash or kind, and remember this - 'Life is what you make it.'"* Indeed, Rigga, as he was affectionally called, instilled strong values in us and also ensured that we were comfortable. His work ethic and care helped to establish a good life for us, and this brought him a lot of joy as a father. He would always declare, *"My children will have a roof over their heads"* and this underscored his lessons of home ownership, protection and security. My siblings and I remain grateful for these spoken words. Today, every one of us own homes. This is not to say, however, that we did not have other challenges while growing up. Housing, however, was never a difficulty for the most part. I am therefore grateful for my father, my coach, who emphasized this as a priority and attainable goal.

Spoken words are powerful. As children of God, our words are life creating (Proverbs 18:21). In realising this, I would print affirmations and place them in my home for my children to read, believe, conceive, and achieve. We were given dominion on the earth to identify our quarterbacks and win! **An awareness of your capacity, challenges, and capabilities are fundamental keys to accepting your call to duty, being resilient, and experiencing more abundance in your life.**

Winning with God at the Centre

A core tenet of my winning strategy is that God should be the centre of our lives. *"For in him we live and move and have our being. As some of your own poets have said, 'We are his offspring'"* (Acts 17:28a, NIV). Accepting that He has created us and trusting that He has the blueprint for our destinies can catalyse us into discovering who we are and what we are called to do. This knowledge can also help us to navigate pitfalls and grow from experiences. It is equally important as you accept the core of your existence to be equipped with the tools or gears required for your fight to win the game.

The Bible story of David and Goliath illustrates how a God-centred life can inspire our confidence and help us defeat the giants in our way. The situation in Israel at that time seemed grim. Goliath had the shout, statue, and status of a ruthless enemy. Yet, be like David the shepherd boy, who had confidence in his God-given capabilities to face Goliath. David was also convicted of his calling and stood courageously despite opposition. He was sickened with disgust to see his people being humiliated by an uncircumcised Philistine and rose with courage to face the giant of his day. He chose to utilise what he was familiar with as a weapon in fighting Goliath. David therefore refused Saul's armour and was victorious in slaying the enemy of his soul, striking him down with a stone that he had in his sling bag. A small stone and a lot of courage caused the giant to fall (1 Samuel 17).

Like David, today we walk with the Rock within us and believe that *"...Greater works than these shall [we] do...."* (John 14:12, KJV). David remained true to himself, trusting his gut to use what he had practiced with a pebble. Faith, as small as a mustard seed, can move mountains (Matthew 17:20-21). As you start this journey of self-actualisation, learning navigation insights, and living a victorious life, do a self-check—**Are you equipped? Are you ready to face your giants?**

Game On!

The story of David and Goliath is compelling because of its applicability to my life. Just as David faced taunts and challenges from his brothers and the giant Goliath, I encountered whispers and criticisms about my attire in the early stages of my career in the corporate world. My co-workers whispered. Goliath shouted with aimless threats, and my General Manager shouted with prudent corrections. Yet, like David, I chose to take a proactive stance, turning the situation into an opportunity that demonstrated my determination and resilience to learn from every opportunity. It is important not to take offence easily. By doing that, you only hurt yourself. See the best in all situations and avoid being bothered at all costs. This is what I did and it enabled me to make the necessary adjustments while maintaining amicable relationships on the job. It was painful and humiliating to go through this experience, but in the end, the giant of embarrassment that came to attack my self-confidence was defeated.

In sports, offense or offence (known as "attack" outside of North America), is "the action of attacking or engaging an opposing team with the objective of scoring points or goals" American Football Database). In David's case, he chose to go on the offence and he defeated Goliath; we would say the rest is history. So, it is with me at that time. I did not realise that I was on the offence but I was determined to score and win in the fight. Providing for my children was my priority and nothing would prevent me from performing my duties. I had left the insurance company that I was working at and this was my second This was my second shot, and I would not lose the opportunity. **Life is what you make it!** A winner therefore attacks problems head-on and finds viable solutions instead of running away.

In this game of life, be therefore reminded to not take offense easily. Maintain focus on your priorities such as providing for your children or improving your skillset. This tenacious spirit exemplifies the importance of staying steadfast in the face of adversity. Viewing challenges as opportunities can therefore help us to discover our inner your strength and resolve. This can propel forward in our endeavours, just as David's offense led to victory.

> **Game Rule #2:**
> It is important not to take offence easily. By doing that, you only hurt yourself.

The attitude of determination and perseverance reflects the belief that life is what you make it. By choosing to approach challenges with a positive mindset and a willingness to act, you empower yourself to overcome obstacles and achieve success. Remaining authentic throughout the game from start to finish is a game-changer in securing the win; grit and gut—**Game on!**

Game Strategies During Interviews

Every job has an application process and we are often competing with many similarly qualified individuals in our fields for fewer job opportunities. After the initial screening process from our application materials, the interview is usually the next step to distinguish ourselves from the other candidates.

Having worked twenty years in one industry, serving the two leading distributors, each with two tenures, I can safely say that acing the interview and securing the job are not easy, but certainly possible. Let me share one example with you.

I had worked for both Company A and Company B, left Company B to work at Company A and was now leaving Company A to back to Company B. This would be my second stint at Company B and was essentially a promotion as it was a managerial position and above my previous roles. During my interview for this managerial role at Company B, I was asked, "What will you say to your customers about representing one brand, then leaving for another?" I responded by demonstrating my preparedness for the interview, loyalty to any brand that I work with and without flickering my belief in my capabilities as a trusted sales professional.

I went on to share a story of an instance during my first tenure at Company A and how this business deal helped me to demonstrate my integrity on the job and the confidence that customers have in me. One of our customers had a service request with a machine they bought from Company B, yet there was delay in response. Word got back to the customer that there was some unwillingness from senior management to expedite the service call. Nonetheless, after returning to Company A, the customer contacted me, and Company A was able to secure the deal from Company B. Importantly, the customer told me that it was because of me why they transferred their business from Company B. They explained that if I was still at Company B they would have kept the business there, but they had confidence in me so they went with the other company. As this transpired, I remained transparent and consistent in all my dealings and explained that if the customer saw me being disloyal to either company, I would not have gained respect or garnered their trust to be their sales representative. They knew that I would pay attention to their needs and therefore followed me with their business to the company that I was serving. When you are authentic and devoted to your craft, business will therefore follow you wherever you go. After that response, in an almost two-hour interview, I was asked, *"When will you be available to start?"* Yes, my friends - **It is possible for you to have good success without selling your soul!**

As you prepare for job interviews, I therefore encourage you to be aware of the industry in which you work and also open to the fact companies are both competitors and colleagues. Clients also trust us to represent their best interests and want to be assured that they are getting value for their money. How then can you win in your interviews and what game strategies can you use? Some winning strategies for interviews are standard across industries. Like anything else that you aspire to be good in, preparedness is the key. Research the background of the company that you are seeking employment. Get a good sense of the company culture, its clients, mission and vision. Look at its success in the market that it operates and also avenues where you see yourself making a meaningful contribution. In other words, be very clear on what you bring to the table. Package yourself and sell yourself well by showing up appropriately attired. Do not be sloppy. Make sure that your outfit is clean, ironed and fit you well. Pay attention to your hygiene. While these may seem like ordinary tasks, do not underestimate the importance of looking and smelling good. Your recruiters should be able to look at you and see you representing the company. The care that you give to your attire can therefore be an indication of the care that you give to business entrusted to your care.

In your interview, unravel the package that you bring to the company by telling your story. Prepare beforehand a narrative of who you are (**your values**), how you came to be who you are today (**your experiences**) and why you do what you do (**your purpose**). Infuse this story with anecdotes and show how your values, experiences and purpose align with the goals of the company. As you tell your story, be also attentive to what is being said to you. The company is trying to find out if you are a good fit for them, but you also need to be sure that this is a good fit for you. Pay attention to how company representatives speak with you. Do they do so with respect? Are they organized? Do they give you a clear job description and proposed start date? What does the compensation package look like? Demonstrate your interest in the company by having at least two questions at the end.

These questions should show your research into the company's work and not focused on you.

As you participate in your interview, know that success often comes down to the intangibles. Once you get your foot into the door for an interview, recruiters already know that you are qualified. The intangibles are often therefore the difference maker. What are some of these? Many companies are also looking for employees who demonstrate trustworthiness, honesty, loyalty and integrity. Business also requires discretion and confidentiality, so companies are also looking for that. As you prepare yourself for interviews, be also aware that if your goal is to win at all costs, then you will come across as inauthentic and this can cause you to miss opportunities that you are otherwise qualified for.

Work hard and pursue opportunities as they present themselves, but never burn your bridges behind you. In your interviews, never talk bad about your previous places of employment. Highlight the growth opportunities that you were exposed to, the mentorship and encouragement that you received, as well as how that job prepared you for the one that you are now seeking. An open, gracious and grateful attitude is by far a better winning strategy than a deceitful and ungrateful one. As you prepare to sell products and services, always remember therefore that you are the first thing that you sell to others, and you do so with confidence and integrity, playing by the rules of the game but never selling your soul.

Game Rule #3:
In interviews, recruiters already know that you are qualified. The intangibles are often what will set you apart.

CHAPTER 2

FINDING COMMON GROUND

"I have learned that people will forget what you said, people will forget what you did, but people will never forget how you made them feel."
Maya Angelou

"Bran thought about it. 'Can a man still be brave if he's afraid?' 'That is the only time a man can be brave,' his father told him."
George R.R. Martin - A Game of Thrones

Quarter Break

Bravery will surface when all odds are against you and you somehow still continue to play and score in the game of life. My life has therefore been one where bravery that I did not know I possessed showed up in times when I felt afraid and uncertain, and also as I received encouragement from others.

As I continued in my career, I was determined to understand more about sales, share in the love of heavy equipment as my father did, and win again. I did, however, take a quarter break to rejuvenate my soul. Life sometimes requires us to take a break, but that does not mean that we are out of the game or that we are losing. Breaks can give us an opportunity to rest, refocus and re-strategize. After a brief hiatus, I was back in the game and in an arena that my father had served.

My father was a tractor driver and would often share with delight his exploits at Alcoa and the many quarries around the country. I was confident that I, being his daughter, his DNA running through my veins would guarantee me smashing the glass ceiling in the heavy equipment industry. It is therefore important to share your passion with others. My father had always shared his heart with anyone in his circles and would gleefully introduce me to his associates as his star daughter. One of such persons was Mr. Harrison. Mr. Harrison was a giant in construction field in the 1970s and 80s. I recall visiting him to share the news of my employment in the industry and he exclaimed how proud my dad would have been to know that I was serving at the company that represented some of the leading brands in heavy equipment.

Indeed, David's words are true in the Psalms when he said, *"I am young and now am old yet I have not seen the righteous forsaken or his children begging bread"* (Psalm 37: 25, ESV). The spoken words of being a star and having the potential to be a force to be reckoned with was like music to my ears as I started in the industry on February 5, 2001. I was convinced that I was walking in my calling, cemented in confidence and courage. Those words that my father had spoken over my life so many years ago had ricocheted from my past, sounded into my present as Mr. Harrison echoed them and vibrated into my destiny. I felt alive and full of purpose as a sense of accomplishment dawned on me. Rigga's star girl was winning in life!

Coaching Tip #2: Write down some positive words that were spoken over your life that you still have not seen come to pass. Put your name in front of them and say them out loud. For example, I, Susan Gordon Kinnane am a star performer in my industry. People actively seek me out because of my expertise. Put these words on your phone, on your wall, or computer and read them every day. You can also record your voice speaking these words and listen to it regularly. These positive words will help you to cancel out the negative voices around you and help you win in life.

The spoken word is very powerful. Both life and death are in your tongue. Use your tongue to speak life and not death over your life, dreams and aspirations.

Honour and Bravery

With determination to excel in the heavy equipment industry, following my father's footsteps was my inspiration. Despite facing challenges and setbacks, I stayed in the game with bravery and a clear goal in mind. My father's legacy and the pride he would have felt seeing me serve in such a prominent company fuelled my determination to succeed. I also want to speak about the role of honour and how this can help us to be brave while staying true to our values. By honour here, I mean integrity and uprightness; sticking to what is right. Boy Scouts, for example, understand this and have an honour code. Honour therefore means that we pay attention to our reputation and that we keep our word. Honour fuels bravery. It is therefore important to establish and emphasize the importance of honour in the early years of rearing, nurturing of our children so that it becomes the norm of children in your family or sphere of influence. This will foster an innate characteristic of bravery which will motivate us to do what is right, even when it is hard. A person who is honourable will daringly play the game as is required, even when the odds are against them.

Bravery and honour require us to draw strength from our faith or anything that centres us. For some of this, this might include finding some quiet time or mediating on the wisdom of the Scriptures. Whatever it is that rekindles the spark in you, find it and use it in those moments when you do not feel brave and are tempted to be dishonourable. One of my favourite things to do is to find comfort in the Psalms. I also go back to my affirmations on a daily basis. These spoken words of encouragement serve as a powerful reminder of who I am the importance of believing in myself. This helps to speak positivity into my existence and thereby shape my reality. You too can use your words to shape your reality, and by speaking affirmations of success and resilience, you empower yourself to overcome obstacles and achieve your goals.

Common Ground

My journey reflects the power of determination, faith, and the spoken word in shaping my destiny. Keep pressing forward with confidence, knowing that you also have the potential to make a significant impact in your industry and beyond.

Reflecting on my experiences in my parent's small shop, being a part of a Century Club, and being awarded Branch Rookie of the Year acted as fuel to my work. I just knew that this new position was pivotal, and if I was effective in playing successfully, it would change the trajectory of my generation. It was even more impactful for me to learn that I was the first female sales representative in the heavy-duty equipment industry in post-independent Jamaica. My company represented several pioneering brands and I was a part of that history. I was like a child in a candy store, ready for the encounters and experiences and to do the work to be successful. This was not a three-card monte card game but one that would require focus, faith, and fortitude.

Each day as I reported to work as a single mother with two children, both under the age of ten, the youngest being ten weeks and the older having sickle cell disease, my primary focus at that moment was food, medical expenses, daycare, educational needs and clothing for my children. One can therefore understand that my attire was not my primary concern. I was on the offence with my passion; I wore it with confidence. I annihilated the whispers, and the narrative in the office started to slowly change to, *"You know the personable, passionate new sales rep with no clothes yet?"* I had a suitcase of confidence and courage. I was determined for the industry to discover my virtuoso in the sales arena and this common ground of efficacy on the job was what we stood on each day, so I persevered during those growing moments.

The whispers became talks. Some persons started to compliment me with words such as, *"You are now looking nice."* Another person said, *"You are improving in your attire."* My response remained constant, *"Conceive, believe it, and achieve it. I am the fashionista around here."* Things were settling down; a couple of months had passed, and each month, I got a few pieces to improve my wardrobe.

Murphy's law is an adage that states, *"Anything that can go wrong will go wrong."* As I was working on improving myself and taking care of my young family, the talks about me continued. The talks had also reached the ears of the CEO who was stationed at our head office. One fateful Monday morning during their monthly management meeting, the matter was discussed. He is allegedly remarked, *"Look at her, she is not suitable to be selling our expensive equipment. Her heel back is dirty, yes, look at her right heel. Please, someone stop that young lady!"*

Those words hurt, but my encounters and experiences have taught me that the process is temporary. It is sometimes painful, but the promise is permanent and sweeter after the trials and sufferings. This, however, was not the only experience that I had that motivated me to work even harder. Heavy equipment sales is an industry that requires personal protective gears (PPE) and safety gears. The basic work garments are pants and flat shoes, but my best outfit in those early days was a red and white polka dot dress. A part of this was due to my gaining employment after a three years' hiatus from working in the corporate world. This gap was due to a series of events including the death of my father, operating a bar and the birth of my second child. I therefore only had a few pieces of clothing suitable for corporate work. The workplace required clothing that would not be a safety hazard and certainly, a long flowing dress was a misfit. The General Manager at that time was a Jamaican Chinese with the driest sarcasm. Whimsically, he exclaimed in frustration as I strolled across the yard to the garage— bear in mind that whenever I wore that dress, I felt like a fashion icon, like I was representing Princess Diana well in Jamaica— *"You do not wear trousers; the dress looks nice yet around here, trousers are required to ensure your safety."* My first lesson from this incident was the feedback sandwich approach. A feedback sandwich is a method of feedback where positive feedback serves as a cushion to negative feedback. Generally, a manager or superior delivers positive feedback. Then, they deliver critical or constructive feedback and close with something feedback. Here, the General Manager complimented my attire, but let me know that it was not the most appropriate because of the safety issues. We therefore shared the common ground that I should do everything to be safe on the job, which included how I dressed for work.

More than a decade before this incident, I was in my early twenties and my branch manager in life insurance coached me into understanding the importance of dressing for your position. Some of the lasting lessons are that clothing must be clean, ironed, and fit well. I have never forgotten this coaching. (If you can recall my interview tips, you will realize that I actually passed on some of what I learned from my branch manager). During my time in insurance, my wardrobe therefore contributed significantly to my confidence as I engaged hundreds of prospects and developed a reputation as a fashionista. I was even a finalist in the company's pageant, where ladies from varying branches displayed talents and wardrobes. While I did not cop the top prize, I was present in all aspects of the competition. The activities enabled me to meet new acquaintances, learn new roles, and reignited a desire to serve the underserved. This happened during one of our visits to an elderly home; I will share more later in the book. At the heavy equipment company, I had to make the adjustment to what was required and this took me some time. I therefore had to pull on my reservoir of memories of the confidence that I was equipped in my previous job to get the required clothing for my new role. As painful as the criticisms were, I had to remind myself that this is not who

Rules of the Game

I am. It is important to guard your heart as you transition to another job with different workplace requirements.

As I continued to adjust to the new job, a sweet senior member of staff suggested that I give up the position and seek to join a team of marketers that roamed from office to office, selling seasonal items that are reasonably priced. Usually, they would visit the office at the end of the month, visit malls, and promote their items. *"You need to be earning now,"* she exclaimed. I knew she meant well; she was terrified that I would not make it in that tough, male-dominated industry. She tried so hard to convince me to seek alternate employment. *"You are persuasive. I have observed you with our customers. Yet, I believe you would excel more in that area and grow faster than if you stayed here."* I responded to her that I was grateful for her kind thoughts; however, I knew in my heart that this is what I should do. I also had the patience to wait as I grew into the role. It is very important to be responsible and not hasty in making decisions regarding one's future.

Maturity and self-awareness are very important in the game of life. Acknowledging observations from others is great, but having confidence in your own skillset is critical in navigating your own career path successfully. One must be steadfast and not easily moved. Affirming your commitment to your current path demonstrates a sense of responsibility in decision-making regarding your future. While it is important to listen to advice from experienced colleagues, ultimately, trusting your instincts and staying true to your passion and goals are vital. In business, one also has to learn patience and discipline in order to wait for the right opportunities. There should also be a willingness to put in the hard work needed for success. By staying focused on your chosen path and believing in yourself, you will be better positioned to overcome obstacles and achieve your professional aspirations.

Empathy and Emotional Intelligence in the Workplace

As I faced the different quarters of my career game, other persons spoke into my life. The second voice which really spoke to me in one of these tough moments is a female senior manager who had attended the meeting where I was derided because of my attire. After the meeting She did a practical demonstration, and this was my first recollection of empathy in the work arena. She asked me to place my right heel against hers and went on to explain that she also drove to work. However, to ensure that her heel was covered, she drove a with a soft shoe. This protected her feet from dirt and the abrasiveness of driving. She suggested that and that I could consider doing the same. As she spoke, she did so with one of the softest voices and held my hands. She went on to advise me that funds were located in the budget to provide uniforms. She asked me if I was willing for her to guide me as I grow accustomed to me my new role. I gladly agreed. She explained that she was relieved that I had agreed to her mentoring me as she had advised the others in the meeting that she would be my mentor and talk with me regarding the matter. This gesture was a game changer in my career development and I remain grateful to her for seeing, hearing and understanding my plight and being sensitive in her approach towards helping me grow in this area. **Empathy is a big deal.**

Empathy indeed plays a significant role in fostering positive relationships and creating a supportive work environment. Recognizing and understanding the needs and feelings of others, as demonstrated by the senior manager, can lead to better communication, collaboration, and overall well-being for everyone involved. It is inspiring to see such acts of empathy in the workplace, as they contribute to a culture of care and understanding, ultimately enhancing productivity and job satisfaction.

My general manager was the third voice who really helped me to change my game strategies on the job. One day, he called me into his office. He had good news. *"I have approved uniform, albeit your position does not include uniform as you are a contractor, which is commission-based, and your earnings are untapped. It is important for you to get trousers for work, so I instructed the team to provide uniform materials. Ensure that you get some trousers ASAP."* His sweet secretary chimed in, *"And dressing for work is not a party. No shiny; shine-less is best."* I smiled on the inside. My lesson from this - **Be a Strategist.**

Avoiding flashy or overly extravagant attire aligns with the notion that less is often more when it comes to professional dress. It is important to be strategic in addressing workplace challenges. Be a leader, like Egbert Chang, in recognizing the need for appropriate attire and taking swift action to provide a solution. He not only ensured my comfort and professionalism, but also contributed to a positive work environment. Collectively responding with solutions to challenges in the workplace underscores the value of strategic thinking and proactive problem-solving in addressing workplace needs and fostering a culture of professionalism.

Then there was the Regional HR Manager. In one conversation with her, I shared my distress and embarrassment due to the truthful yet scathing remarks about my attire. She taught me my first lesson in emotional intelligence. *"Rules are written; you abide. Sling back shoe is not appropriate for your work,"* she reminded me. *"You are expecting me to reprimand my CEO for what he said? Girl, he has the authority to pull you from the team or obstruct your play. Stay focused and play."* Angie went on to say, *"Girl, rise to the occasion. Report to duty each day, delivering on that commitment you made during your interview."* —**Emotional intelligence is necessary.**

The insight gained from this experience has taught me a lifelong lesson about the power dynamics within the organization, particularly regarding the CEO's authority. It highlights the importance of recognizing and respecting hierarchical structures while navigating workplace dynamics. Emotional intelligence requires one to understand and control their feelings while also recognizing and understanding the feelings of others. This can be tough when one is feeling hurt, but success in the work place and other relationships depends on it. Success comes as we manage our feelings, stay focused and committed to our duties. Despite the challenges that you face, take the voices of encouragement as they come, be resilient and remain professional. Emotional intelligence and appropriate professional conduct provide insights for navigating workplace challenges with resilience and integrity.

> **Game Rule #4:**
> Emotional intelligence and appropriate professional conduct can help us navigate workplace challenges with resilience and integrity.

Finally, as I reflect on the difficult meeting, there was this other female who said nothing. When she walked out of that room that momentous day, I saw the pain and shame in her eyes. It was a long walk from the boardroom to her office. Even as I write this memoir, it is like I am in that moment: her shoulders were squared, she walked slowly with her eyes filled with pain, and her head was slightly bent so as not to look in my face. When she saw me, it was like she saw a ghost. She was horrified for me. She bravely walked slowly to her desk and continued working diligently. She was the only other female manager in the company at that time. At that moment, I felt like roaring as I watched her walk to her desk, but I did not. I stayed in position – literally and figuratively. Reader, once a seat has been provided for you at the table, stay in position. In the presence of your enemies, eat the six-course meal provided by your Creator and Lord (Psalm 23:5, The Message).

Michelle became my role model as I recognised that she was a confidential person too. She never repeated to me or anyone in my hearing my humiliation, yet there was an unspoken sympathy that I felt from her. She was the poster girl for the organisation, reporting to her duties with discipline and diligence. She remained focused. She was sympathetic to my situation - a young female in the room when the scathing remark was issued, yet she guarded her soul. Truth be told, there was no reason for her to take on the offence. So many times, people project their grievances or issues with others. At other times, some individuals unwarily take on other people's offences. To this day, Michelle continues to serve with the optimum dedication, diligently paying attention to her own affairs. My role model taught me a life lesson, *"Me deh yah fi drink milk, nuh count cow"* (Jamaican proverb). It underscores the importance of focusing on your own actions and responsibilities rather than getting caught up in other's issues or grievances. It is a valuable lesson in emotional maturity and maintaining perspective in challenging situations. You might be playing a game, and a team member receives a card or call. This may or may not be deserving and can affect the outcome of the game. Emotional maturity is therefore critical. A disciplined player sticks to the game plan and finishes strong. Similarly, someone on the job should remain in position and finish the game. **Position yourself in the game to win and remember your core tenets. Be tactical and remain strong!**

Character and resilience are critical in finding your footing in the game. It is likely that one will witness other's struggle and humiliation, yet one must maintain composure and continue to fulfil responsibilities with discipline and diligence. Your ability to handle the situation with grace and confidentiality while offering unspoken sympathy demonstrates strength of character. Exemplify professionalism and integrity. Focusing on your own duties and refusing to take on the offense meant for others highlights emotional maturity and wisdom.

In summary, in finding common ground, it is important to stay true to your principles and remain focused on your goals, even in the face of adversity. By staying tactical, tough, and committed to our tenets, we can navigate through difficult circumstances and emerge stronger on the other side. With bravery untapped, your brand will be a revered, and you will emerge as an indomitable team player.

CHAPTER 3

GIVER OR TAKER?

"Life's persistent and most urgent question is, 'What are you doing for others?"
Martin Luther King

Our father gave all he could to provide a roof for us and served his community. He was a hard worker and a trailblazer in his field. Rigga created a wonderful life for us in the 1980s as he operated a business that was a lucrative, popular hotspot in town. Most celebrities of the 1960s and 70s from Trench Town visited the club; Barry Heptone, Marcia Griffiths, Judith Mowatt, Ken Boothe, and Dobby Dobson were among a few of the greats who were companions of my father from his Trench Town days. These friendships were forged because of him always courageously being a friend to those close to him. He was always supporting others. All he did in that time of play was to show up for others, not expecting anything in return but their support. He lived such a life of service that at his funeral, the constant truth that echoed was about his gregarious giving and selfless service to family and friends.

Thursdays and Sundays were the popular days at the club; melodious old hits were featured on Thursday and Sunday evenings as rock steady and R&B were played. Until this day, "Lady in Red" is one of my favourite songs from that era. Whenever I hear that song, it takes me to that Sunday evening in 1986 when I first heard that song and saw the smiles on the faces of the patrons in the pub… This song definitely brings back a lot of nostalgic feelings. I was also exposed to the dark runnings of a club; drugs, frolicking, and booze. I was a young teenager, very observant and inquisitive. I paid attention when it was in my view and realised early that there were negative consequences for getting involved in drugs and booze.

A police station was in close proximity to the pub, and they were the largest clientele. We also had university staff and students as regular patrons. At the University of the West Indies (UWI), many students who wanted an experience of the night life scene would visit "Ashanti," which was the name of the Pub. I can now appreciate the meaning of the word "Ashanti." It means gratitude and thanksgiving (Bagg, 2024). The vibes and ambiance of the club mirrored those words "joy and bliss." An amazing network was established, and today, graduates of that era are renowned in varying professions including law, medicine, and geology. I mention these three because I hear their names mentioned on the news or read about their activities in the news. I recall their days at UWI, coming over to my parents' establishment having their meals or drinks and rejoice at their level of success.

Our community was sometimes challenged by young men having run ins with the law. Daddy was always willing and able to support them with bail based on his relationships with persons in the security forces. My father knew lawyers, doctors, Indians, and chiefs. I observed my father's interactions and the relief in the mother's face when her boy returned home or the drink of celebration that my dad had with the arresting officer afterwards. I saw in those situations three characteristics which helped to define who I am today: **dedicated, determined and diligent.**

My father's community was always willing to support him in rendering assistance. This speaks to **dedication**; the dedication of my father as a civically engaged citizen, as well as the dedication of the community which was committed to communal support. The mother's love for her child in trouble personifies **determination**. She knew that her child needed help and went to find someone who she knew could. She was determined to see change in her child's story. My father's approach in resolving the issue exemplifies **diligence**. Like King Solomon, he would wisely manage the issue presented before him and pursue the best outcome for all parties involved. Interestingly, as I reflect on the course of my life, I realize how these qualities these qualities surfaced when I faced challenging times. Dedication, diligence, and determination are therefore fundamentals from my formative years. These traits along with my father's example were my fire to do well in my studies so that I could be equipped to be an effective member of the community. I was therefore inspired to do well in all that I do, but to always give back to the community. Daddy was always helping and would often say to us, "You cannot allow a wounded soldier to die." The shouts for help from our neighbours as they called on "Mr. Fish" or "Rigga Fish" therefore became a way of life for us. Through these experiences, we came to understand service, compassion, and care for humanity.

Amidst your fire and zeal to do good in life, there will at times be flames that can cause combustions. If one is not careful, these can cause convulsions and the premature outing of the fire within you. As a teenage girl, the need for fashionable clothing was one such flicker that resulted in discontentment and erosion of my confidence. At that time, we had limited clothes and the ones that we had were not very fashionable. I felt discontented because my peers wore the latest fashion while we did not have many pieces. Life shows, however, that despite the many curve balls and thunderbolts, that is not the end of the game.

My beloved Aunt Daphne, who owned a clothing store, would always support our parents with clothing for my siblings and me. For school uniforms, special holidays, and occasions, Aunt Daphne could be counted on for that. On the other hand, for social occasions, Carolyn, a then young Caribbean School of Media and Communication (CARIMAC) student, would always take gifts for us during her trips from her homeland in California. Two other defining characteristics were shaped in me by their acts of kindness: **compassion and charity.** Both Aunt Daphne and

Carolyn understood our situation and had compassion on us. Their kindness was also charitable as they willingly gave to us to meet our needs. Today, I am very sensitive to those around me who have needs that I am able to meet. I refer where I am going from and the uncomfortable feelings of lack. I am often moved by those who need assistance and try my best to help or point them to others who might be able to better assist.

Interestingly, if one should ask about a defining moment in my life, I would say my teenage years when I realised that we had less than others. I vowed in my heart then that I would provide clothing for my siblings. I would share with my siblings that when I grow up, I would be living in a white townhouse, with an SUV parked outside, a rich husband, three children and, of course, someone to help in the house as I cannot cook. I made those declarations and meant every word. At age thirty-one, I bought my first apartment, owned a ten-year-old Suzuki Vitara, and was living with four children: two of them biological, a nephew, and a cousin. They were all my children; the ages of the children ranged from 4, 10, 14 and 16.

Setting a vision for your future, despite challenges, and working tirelessly to make it a reality are critical for winning. You can make your dreams become a reality just as I did. Owning my first apartment at age thirty-one and providing for four children is fulfilment of a childhood dream; a dream that I was determined to make a reality. Giving is in my DNA. I have been deeply blessed by the opportunity to love and care for my siblings, nephew, and cousin by considering them as my own children. It was not always easy, but definitely a joy to do. Just writing this feels so good all over. Give and stretch; it is in the stretching that you discover your greatest strength.

You too will have a story to tell as a testament to the power of perseverance, vision, and unconditional love. Your story will be an inspiration to others who may be facing similar challenges, showing that with determination and hard work, dreams can indeed come true. Life certainly rewards us when we are more willing to give rather than taking.

> **Game Rule #5:**
> Give and stretch; it is in the stretching that you discover your greatest strength.

The Book of Rules

Book of Rules by The Heptones was one of favourite songs in the 1980s. During high school while other girls in my age group loved Whitney Houston's "Girls Just Wanna Have Fun" I had a different taste in music. The lyrics of "Book of Rules" spoke to me:

"Just like common people like you and me
We'll be builders for eternity
Each is given a bag of tools
A shapeless mass and the book of rules."

Indeed, while we are common people, we can do uncommon things. All of us have gifts, talents and abilities that make up our "bag of tools." Our lives are shaped by what we do with our "tools" and these actions last into eternity. As we build and shape the "mass" of our lives, we therefore have to ensure that we play by "the book of rules."

Other songs also resonated with me. On days when my reality tempted me to feel melancholic, Bob Marley's "Three Little Birds" was my happy song. Yes, I was resolved not to "worry about a thing, 'cause every little thing [was] gonna be alright." Having recognised that education was a means to "making every little thing alright", I strove to make every day count during high school. Education was a catalyst for me to be able to do more for my family. Daddy always emphasized that education was our way out of the village and he was right. I started high school with a sense of purpose; I was a lover of life and progress.

In 7th grade, I was nominated as a Student Councillor. This was a dream come true. I was now on track to being a solution as my daddy encouraged us to be. This nomination helped to validate my voice of advocacy on behalf of issues that concern myself, my peers and siblings. One problem that I was determined to solve was for my sisters and me to be adorned in nicer clothing and to increase our uniforms from two sets to five sets per week. Resilience, ambition, and a strong sense of familial responsibility shaped my determination to overcome obstacles and create a better future for us through education. But I also needed a job.

My father asked one of his patrons for a summer job and I landed my first job at the Ministry of Labour—National Insurance Scheme (NIS) Division. I experienced an epiphany at that moment, I knew that wearing high heels and driving beyond Mona's Aqueduct were my way of life. I went shopping for myself and siblings with my first pay check. It was exhilarating and enthralling. The allure of dressing up, meeting people, and receiving a cheque was invigorating. I was exposed to the trappings of the world and decided in the summer of 1997 that the corporate world was my destiny. This was at age fourteen when I got that first summer job and since then, I have never ceased to make my contribution to the working class. I had a glimpse of what I wanted my future to be and I kept taking active steps towards it. It is therefore important in parenting, family life, and business to be a giver of ideas. Share experiences that can motivate people to dream and pursue their goals. Usually, if persons can see something, they will believe it is possible. Shirley Chisholm shared her dream to be President of the United States of America decades ago and today Kamala Harris is serving as Vice President, making her the first woman, first black American and first South Asian-American to do so. Among her many firsts is also the fact that she is of Indian-Jamaican heritage. In the Jamaican context, The Honourable Portia Simpson-Miller has the distinction of being the first female Prime Minister. These are just a few examples of trailblazing women who have etched their days in history. Millions of girls around the world are inspired by their example and are encouraged that nothing is impossible if they just believe.

Giving Within the Family

A summer job at that time was not only a means of making money, but was also an escape a turbulent season in our family. Those were tough times for us both emotionally and financially because my father lost the establishment. He was betrayed by a friend who bought the club that went up for sale right under my father's nose. We were literally kicked out of Ashanti and given three months to vacate. History has a way of repeating itself, as daddy would often share. After my father's father died, his mother lost the family home. This resulted in him and his siblings being displaced. They were split up among family members. He was shipped to his aunt in St. Thomas, and he would recall that those were the best years of his life. He often said, *"The ones I spent with my cousins, Horace, Burchell, and Dolly; they were the best years of my life."*

Two things happened while my father spent his formative years with his aunt; he recognised the value of attending a Bible-believing church and he also learned the value of a good education. Do not be afraid to give your children a view of your life, the struggles you endured and also your moments of triumph. This can enable them to make informed decisions about their future. It is also important for relatives to know each other. Daddy gave me the joy of knowing Rev. Horace Russell, a pioneer in education and the Baptist church. He was my father's first cousin. I felt proud knowing greatness ran through my blood. As Russell recounts his childhood, he talks about many happy moments. *"We never knew we were poor,"* he would often say. Amidst it all, our parents also gave us the same experience. We did not have everything that we wanted, but we had everything that we needed. Looking back, my siblings and I always echoed the sentiment, *"We never knew we were poor."*

Trevor "Rigga" Gordon had guts and grit. He pushed through Trench Town, cutting sugarcane on UWI Estate, driving a tractor at Quarries or Alcoa, and serving the people of his community and family. We were often last in the line. It was, however, for a worthy cause, as he ensured that we always had a roof over our heads. While there are other things that he could have focused on as a parent, housing and protection were his priorities. He therefore owned a home and gave us the security and sacredness of that space because he did not have it as a child. He ensured he gave it to "his generation"—as he would refer to us back then—and I am so glad he did.

Family is the first place of socialisation. It is therefore important in shaping our values and passing on traditions. I observed my father calling his older sisters "Sister Pearly," "Sister Daphne," and his older brother "Brother Stephen." He also loved and cared for his younger siblings, Claire, Leggy and Bunny. As children, we had to address our elders as "Miss" or "Mister", "Aunt" or "Uncle". There was no malice in our home. *"Cleanliness is godliness. The yard had to be clean for the Spirit of God to reign,"* my dad would say. I grew up in a home where we served each other, and today, I live my life in the same way. I still show respect to my elders even though I am now grown and teach my children to do the same.

Instilling respect and care for family members fosters a deep sense of community and responsibility and helps to root us in this world. Cleanliness and service are also important as we aim to be effective givers. These values can be passed down through generations and affect the way we interact with others. They also shape our approach to life.

Rigga gave it his all, down to wire. He lost it all and courageously regained it. To date, his setup (night before his funeral) celebration was one of the largest our community has ever seen. There were cars parked as far as the Post Office, which is about five miles of parked cars. Courage, greatness, kindness, and loyalty run through my bloodline. **I am wired to win; nothing is impossible!** Whatever life throws at me, I am therefore confident that I can "Put in a punch", which is an expression that my father used to say to me when he wanted to encourage me work harder or complete a task. He was a giver, not a taker in this life and I also endeavour to do the same.

The mention of Rigga's journey, from loss to triumph, and the immense celebration that followed is a testament a life well-lived. My family's experiences have instilled a belief in me that nothing is impossible. I also have a fierce determination to overcome obstacles and achieve success.

My commitment to serving others and willingness to "put in a punch" reflect my readiness to face challenges head-on and positively impact my community. This the strong foundation upon which I stand. With a strong mindset, you too can ensure the continuity of legacy, courage, greatness, kindness, and loyalty in your family, just as in mine.

Coaching Tip #3: In what ways can you become a more effective giver? What needs have you observed in your family, community or workplace? What resources do you have that might help you to meet these needs? Write down these needs on a sheet of paper and your resources on another. Identify one of these needs that you can realistically meet and match it with at least one of your resources. Give yourself a timeline in which you will meet that need. Put a check mark at the need after you meet it and make plans to address some of the others on your list.

As you become a more strategic and effective giver, you may also realize that you may need the support of others to meet some of your goals. Look around for community clubs, volunteers and workplace initiatives that align with your goals and team up with them. Some projects may be for the long term, while others may be shorter. Some may also require more resources and your involvement more than others. Choose your project wisely, but always aim to do something. Exercising your giving muscle while you continue to live your life on purpose will help to foster a spirit of generosity within you which can be the spark for others to come along.

Paying it Forward

"Someone once said every man is trying to either live up to his father's expectations or make up for his father's mistakes."
—**Barak Obama, The Audacity of Hope**

This saying has been my truth and contributed to how I intentionally engage individuals I have met along my journey. Some years ago, I saw an elderly man in the foyer of my office who waiting for an extended period of time; he was waiting to meet with our HR Officer. He went on to explain that his son was working at our office as an intern; however, his internship would expire soon and he was beseeching the company to keep him in our employment as the community that he was living in was likely to lure him into crime and he would end up being an unemployed, high-risk child.

As I listened to the man, I recalled that moment at fourteen years old when my father asked our neighbourhood shopkeeper, Judy, to assist me with a summer job, and how my life changed because of it. The work experience at fourteen years old was like a glimpse into the future that I could have. As I mentioned earlier, I realised that there was more to life than my present circumstances. I saw before the possibility and power of wearing high heels, straight skirts, tailored shirts, and receiving an income. The feeling was euphoric, and I was resolute that this would be my way of life. At fourteen years old, I knew the corporate world would be my way of life. Just as the Lord placed stars in the skies, my earthly father nicknamed me "Star". This was my moment to pay it forward by negotiating on this father's behalf. The HR Officer gave his word to the father, and up to the time of writing, the young man is still employed to that company. The recruit was made aware of his father's petition on his behalf, and I encouraged him to live up to his father's expectations **and whispered to myself "As I'm living up to mine."**

As you aim to win in the game of life, be aware that you will also be required to pay it forward. I knew from an early age where I wanted to be as a career, but I needed someone to speak on behalf and also for someone to give me the opportunity to work. Reflecting on this knowledge encouraged me to speak on the young man's behalf. It was now my turn to pay it forward. You too must be willing and deliberate to pay it forward by negotiating on behalf of others. While I spoke on the young man's behalf, his first advocate was really his father, just as my father was for me. I did, however, recognize that I also had a role to play. I recalled the times that empathy was shown to me and also my commit to helping others succeed. By encouraging the young man to live up to his father's expectations, I was really pulling on traditions of honouring family values and responsibilities. Playing this role was very rewarding. In some ways, the euphoria I felt was like a batsman who hits

Rules of the Game

a ball for six in a game of cricket. Being a giver and not a taker will help you continue in the game for a long time. This, and other similar experiences can also happen to you as you pay it forward.

CHAPTER 4

CONNECTING

"History will be kind to me for I intend to write it."
Sir Winston Churchill

"Confidence is a sense of certainty in our own abilities."
Brené Brown

Empathy and shared experiences go a long way in fostering connection and belonging. When we recognize that each person carries their own burdens and experiences, this allows for greater understanding and compassion in our interactions with them. Loss, in particular, has a profound way of bringing people together and creating bonds that transcend individual differences. Whether it is the loss of a loved one or any other kind of loss, the desire to fill the void left behind can drive people to seek connection and support from others.

Outside of loss, moments of difficulty and frustration can also help us connect with others. Often, our previous experiences or knowledge can become the solution to somebody's problem. This highlights the power of empathy and support in building resilience and overcoming challenges. By sharing our journeys and connecting with others, we find solace and support and cultivate confidence, consistency, and courage.

The bustling activity at the dealership's parts counter during the early 2000s is a vivid example of how shared experiences such as purchasing original parts can serve as a unifying force within a community. It was, and still is today, a testament of the importance of relationships and connections in both personal and professional settings. **This mindset creates confidence, consistency, and courage to share one's journey and connect with others.**

Having accepted a new position as Parts and Service Sales Manager at a company that I served at before, I knew it was important to have a good understanding of the issues and connect with all stakeholders. I therefore sought to have dialogue with our staff, and especially our customers. There was one customer who was a little more expressive than others about his needs. He did not hide his joy if he was satisfied, neither did he conceal his displeasure if he was unhappy with our service. Yes, Mangalo from St. Mary would give out shouts of hallelujahs when the service pleased him, but he would also release several choice words from his repertoire of Jamaican curse words if he was dissatisfied.

We met at his garage in St. Mary and had an open conversation about how we can better meet his needs. He shared with me an outline of our enterprise, why he had purchased a particular brand's machine, and what he required from the dealership. He encouraged me to accept the challenge of the new position and to always endeavour to understand the "why" for our the stakeholders. Thank you, Mangalo. Thank you for giving me the opportunity to connect with you and to grow in my role as a Parts and Service Sales Manager. May your wise counsel continue to enrich the lives of others and bring your children divine blessings (see Isaiah 44:3).

Three years in, and the honeymoon was over. The paradox that the darkest rooms create the best photographs became my truth as the company was underperforming (bleeding from losses). The word in the meetings describing our affairs was "haemorrhaging". Four months before this, we had a significant layoff; over forty persons were made redundant. The staff was trying to wrap their heads around all that was happening as we planned an end-of-year activity. I suggested to the management team that we could have Christmas outings to create fellowship and motivation for the new year. Out of this suggestion, the company's annual Christmas Family Day was birthed. This involved employees and family members coming together and has become a successful company tradition. There are opportunities in every situation. This event was a catalyst for change. Our message to the staff was that, albeit the bottom line is showing negative growth, we value you and your family. We were inspired to face the headwinds of the new year together, and we knew that this could only be achieved with a strong team. The chain is indeed as strong as its weakest link.

Confidence to Win

It was a gloomy afternoon in February 2014 when we received the news that our company was underperforming and we needed a turnaround plan by September 2014. Staff morale had increased since our Christmas Family Day and we had established targets for improving. It was therefore disheartening to get the news that things were so bad that if there was no turnaround, it would be all over for us. In that moment, I came to the sobering reality that the estimated 60 persons in the After-Sales Department and their families were depending on what I did as a senior management team member: swim or sink! They were my responsibility. My mind swung into action. I remembered whose daughter I was. I am the daughter of a survivor, Rigga Fish. I started my training for this day from the age of seven when I assisted my parents in counting empty bottles and paying customers for their returns. By age eight, I was always a part of the stocktaking process in the shop. I was aware of the Pareto 80/20 rule: 20% of the customers gave us 80% of the revenues, and it was important to know who those customers were.

The credit book, as Mommy would call it, had the customers' names and balances that would contribute to significant sales. Whenever we had customer appreciation parties, the special customers were first on the invitation list. This was important to my parents as these customers were staunch supporters, as my father often referred to them. Customer satisfaction was critical to us as we built customer loyalty during my father's comeback strategy from the fallout in the late 1980s. Rest assured, he did pivot and expand in the 1990s. One of the contributing factors to the rebound and success of my late father's business was the appreciation that the patrons felt as they supported the business. Others often talk about the communal feeling that they had as they hung out under the mango tree nearby.

Recently I was having a conversation with a patron who visited the bar in those days. He explained that he was actually under the mango tree at my father's bar enjoying a cold Heineken as the news commentator announced the shooting incident involving Jeff "Free I" Dixon and Peter Tosh. This incident shocked the music industry and is still remembered because of Peter Tosh's contribution to reggae. Many other patrons have related remembering being by my father's bar when some significant event occurred. The pub was meeting place for people to socialize, listen the news and engage in social commentary. Great music, food, and fellowship characterized those settings. Each customer felt special as music was selected to their individual taste and meals were prepared to order. Those were some good days. So it was with me. I wanted to understand the needs of our customers who wanted parts and service. I wanted us to deliver solutions that connected with their needs so that individuals could feel and appreciate the service we provided. I also wanted us to experience high customer satisfaction so that the company could grow in brand loyalty. Connection is very important for good success. Customers must feel a sense of belonging if they are to remain loyal to our business.

I decided to venture on that journey within six months with the objective of growing revenues and increasing customer engagement and satisfaction. It was very important to write the plan. Jimmy Cliff's song "The Harder They Come, became one of my favourite hits. I fully believed that the harder those problems came, the harder they would fall. I also held on to the words of Winston Churchill - *"History will be kind to me as I intend to write it."*

Each unit manager was encouraged to connect with their teams, foster creativity, chart a course for improving our scores, and get ourselves out of the hole. Each team member was assigned a learning plan; customer targets were divided among the team, along with objectives for improving the common denominator: our customers were not connected to us. In many ways, our engagement with them was transactional, but our customers wanted to feel seen, heard and cared for. They wanted to be assured that we had the capacity and capabilities to service their needs in a thoughtful way.

> **Game Rule #6:**
> Customers must feel a sense of belonging if they are to remain loyal to our business.

As far back as ten years old, I recognised the importance of responding to person's needs. We had two dance groups at our and there was always the contention about which is the better dancing group. Unbeknownst to my parents and our elders, I planned and staged a dance contest in the open land close to my home. I also provided sandwiches and other refreshments. It was a fun-filled time with games and the dance competition closed the session. The winning group was led by my friend Jacqui and today, decades later, she is still one of the best dancers that I know. I believe that in some ways, that competition stirred something in her and motivated her to further hone her skills as a dancer. For me, whenever I have an opportunity to plan a conference or meeting, I recall the small ten year old girl who organised that successful Fun Day and dancing competition and remind myself that I am capable of greatness.

One of my niches in business is the ability to anticipate and respond to what our customers need. Some of this came from watching my father. My father as an astute businessman had the insight to invest in an alternate source of energy—a generator, or a "Delco" as we call it in Jamaica. This was during the 1980s. By the time Hurricane Gilbert occurred, he owned the plant and was able to provide entertainment to the community and iron school uniforms for our family and close friends. Through the parties, my family earned extra income, and it was out of that period in 1989 that I saw Rigga rise like a Phoenix and started to move progressively. In and around that same period, my dad renamed his sound system "Progressive Disco." Daddy was back in the game—a conqueror. I learned from the best.

My father entered the last decade of his life in the 1990s as a building contractor. He was making and supplying blocks to a nearby housing development. The generator was rented by other sound owners, and Dad also invested in the racehorse business. He had multiple streams of income and we witnessed his triumphant completion of our family home. This provided me and my siblings with our own bedrooms and bathroom amenities. I learned from this the value of endurance. **Enduring the process is required for one to effectively prepare to receive the promise of their dreams.**

Now back to our company and the crisis it was facing. We embarked on a journey where all stakeholders would come out as victors. Our customers needed the assurance that our company was able to secure their investments and our employees needed the confidence that customers perceived them as a trusted provider in the industry. Our team embarked on a connection drive with our customers. Now that I look back, in many ways, we were ahead of some of the online initiatives that our company now uses to source parts. We had a sales blitz. The entire team was singing "Hit the Road, Jack". Our Country Director used this song to motivate us and it became our anthem as we hit the road. The entire sales team blanketed the island, visiting customers onsite, classified them, reviewed their needs and segmented our solutions as per their respective requirements. These solutions were tailored for each customer with a strategic action plan during a seminar.

The seminar provided the opportunity for us to showcase our local talents to build the customers' confidence in our team. Our suppliers also sent Brand Representatives, who presented on the different products and services, highlighting why customers should stay connected to their authorised local dealership. The seminar was a resounding success on a budget of less than JA$50,000. Jamaica is forever grateful to Jaco Nolte for buying into the vision and sponsoring the dream. Together with the win, we found a way. Today, that customer seminar continues to be a strategic action plan of connecting with customers within the dealership.

In the second year of the seminar, my confidence had grown so much that I produced a seven-minute testimonial of the dealership's offerings. This video was done on a very low budget, but the engagement with it was high. Our team members, including Myron, a forty-year veteran in the service field who is very respected and connected in the industry were all featured. They showcased the dealership along with its product and service offerings. The video was a hit.

We were on a roll; history was kind to us as by the customer seminar in 2018, we had done two subsequent videos. The testimonials highlighted the capabilities of the dealership and its contribution to nation-building. Our suppliers were made aware of our video and supported creating a customer testimonial. This captured our partnership with an established local company as they embarked on and successfully executed an initiative of self-generated electricity on the island. This allowed us to connect even more with our clientele. Today, a customer testimonial of the partnership is in the archives of our suppliers' parent company.

The experience in 2014 taught us a lot about confidence and connection and how they can help us win in the game of life. Confidence in the capabilities of the team to rise to the occasion allowed us to find an innovative approach to connecting with customers through sales blitzes and tailored solutions. We were also united in our approach. Demonstrating a proactive and customer-centric mindset is critical for good success in the game and we held on to that strategy. The turnaround plan of the customer seminar, organized on a modest budget also highlights the power of collaboration and strategic planning in achieving impactful results. Much can be done even with limited resources if we are creative and intentional about our goals. During the seminar, we saw Jamaica's vibrant culture and local talents

Rules of the Game

being showcased and this built confidence in the team. This display also fostered stronger relationships with our customers and suppliers, which made us even more connected in our mission.

As you pursue your life goals, connect with your culture and be adaptable to change and new ideas. Perseverance, adaptability, and collaboration are needed to achieve success. As your forge connections in the workplace and elsewhere, be cognizant of the fact that the practice of connection starts in your family. Be deliberate in knowing your siblings or other family members. Be aware of their challenges and interests and if possible, how you can work together to advance your family's legacy. There is a Jamaican proverb that admonishes us to *"learn fi dance a yard before you guh abroad."* This speaks to us practising different behaviours at home before we do them publicly. Our attempts at confidence and connection should therefore be done in the home before we do them elsewhere. Embracing these values of confidence and connection will pave the way for continued growth and prosperity.

Coaching Tip #4: Take a moment to reflect on where you are now in your studies, workplace or community. How connected are you with the people you serve or who are on the same journey with you? What can you do to improve the sense of belonging that people feel around you? If you are studying and are a part of a group, how can you encourage each study group partner to play their role? If you are in the workplace, how can you inspire your team to know your customers or clients better? How can you help to increase community spirit where you live?

Reflect on the patterns of connection that your learned while growing up. This may take you some time. How did you feel close to someone? Was it when you shared a meal? Was it during a conversation? Was it when you did some activity together? Write down the ways in which you feel connected and identify how you can replicate them where you are now. Do the same thing with confidence. How did you learn to be confident? Was it through something that was said to you? Was it by doing something over and over? Take a look at the people you work or serve with. How do they feel confident? Use what you observe to help you better connect and inspire confidence in your teams.

THE SECOND HALF

SHIFT!

"We must shift our thinking away from short-term gain toward long-term investment and sustainability, and always have the next generations in mind with every decision we make."
Deb Haaland

The year was 2000. The millennium year. I was pregnant with my second child and struggled with the meagre returns from the business establishment I was operating to support my daughter, a new baby on the way and myself.

Fried fish and breadfruit were favourites on Friday nights and the weekends when we were organizing Round Robin parties. I was usually in the kitchen on those nights. During my downtime, I would often read books. These books were usually inspirational or focused mainly on business trends.

Susan Gordon Kinnane

I was at my lowest. I had left the insurance industry in 1998 and my beloved father passed away in 1999 after a period of sickness. My finances were depleted. The only thing that I had left was my confidence that I am a conqueror over my circumstances and that I would re-enter the corporate world as soon as I had my son. I knew without doing an ultrasound that it was a boy and I was resolute that I had to shift my perspective and position.

My mother, Delores Leslie, stood with me during the toughest times of my life. She was a creative and diligent homemaker who also worked outside the home as a seamstress. She was kind, quiet, resilient and strong. During those challenging days of my life, I experienced my mother's greatest sacrifice. Owning a motor vehicle is a requirement for any sales position and my beloved mother saved the day; she selflessly gave me her car to "start life" as she referred to it and indeed my life shifted gear. It shifted from the barriers of lack to break free into abundance. Mommy was and still is very kind. She always encouraged us to share our food, time and anything else we had that could help others. This caused us to shift our attention from our circumstances to focus on how we could be of use in the world. One instance of this is Ms. Baker, an elderly lady who many in the community considered to be a little grumpy. She had no friends and no children. Yet, my mother would religiously send her meals every evening. Over time, such a bond was forged between her and our family that my big sisters Dawn and Sandra became her hairdressers.

Rules of the Game

Delores Leslie was soft spoken and through her I learned how potent even soft-spoken words could be. She did not shout, but she was stern and the disciplinarian of the home. My mother did not take kindly to harsh words or rough speaking and always chided us to speak properly. Indeed, she represented the saying, "Loud does not mean strong or quiet, weakness." Like a lioness watching over her cubs, my mom stood with me as a young teenage mother, supporting and caring for my daughter. Nine years later when I became a single mother again, she still stood with me. She never wavered in her support, but always encouraged me to shift my attention to the positives in life. I recall her wanting to come into the delivery room with me during the birth of my son and the nurse said, "No mommy, only the mother." In those moments as I was being coached to give birth to the next generation, I looked into her eyes, the eyes of the one who gave birth to me and garnered strength. Today, my son and my daughter carry in their bodies the legacy of both of my parents. My daughter's name means, "Advisor", while my son's name means, "King". My son also has "Trevor Gordon" as his middle names, which is a tribute to my father. I see in both of them the sternness and kindness of my mother and the tenacity of my father. Their births have helped me to shift my focus and make more decisions that affect the long-term.

Delores, or Beverly as she is also called, migrated to the United States after she reckoned that her children and grandchildren had passed the worst. Over the last 25 years, she has carved a successful life for herself. She is now happily married to her beloved, Calvil. She too, is an example of how one can shift from loss to find love and purpose again.

The lessons that I learned from my mother have lasted me a lifetime. During an interview for a position in motor vehicle sales, the interviewer asked me what are my whys. I shared three things; confidence in my abilities based on my success in life and the industry, my experience around vehicles and the network established through my parents being in business, and having the responsibility to support my then widowed mom, nine-year-old daughter and three (3) month old baby. I clinched by sharing that I was so resolute that I would be successful that I invited my mother along with the baby and they were both downstairs waiting for me. The interviewer asked me how soon I could start. She was also kind enough to accompany me to the car to see the boy as she looked into those bright eyes. She often reminds me that he became her boy forever and indeed, time has honoured her word; Angie has never spoken to me and not asked for her beloved Malik.

Marva Johnson, or "Leitha" as she is also known, is another person who helped me to shift in my career development. She had a budding recruiting agency and successfully placed me for my interviews in the insurance and heavy equipment industries. The shift in gear in my professional career was facilitated by this woman's trust in my capabilities to move products. "Sell," she implored me during our briefing as she shared details of the interview for sales at the Benz dealership. In the end, I was not assigned to the Benz passenger cars location but to the heavy equipment location. This decision shifted me into the greatest assignment of my professional career.

"Leitha" and I go way back. I have always admired her poise and command of the English Language. She is also a close friend of my family, hence she never hesitated in recommending me. She told she knew that I was raised with good morals but that I should always remember that whilst she may have found me the job, it was only I with a good attitude will keep the job. Leitha's belief in me has helped me shift into an industry that would transform my life for many years. Clearly identifying my whys was instrumental as I embraced my shift. What are your whys? What motivates you to do what you do? Knowing the answer to this question will be critical for your success. Knowing your whys can help you to make decisions that will shape your destiny. My mother, Marva and the HR manager all made decisions to that enabled my growth and shifted me into the greatest quarter of my life. What decisions are you making today? Be very deliberate about them as not only will they determine your tomorrow, but will also affect the next generation.

CHAPTER 5

VALUES

"Speak your truth quietly and clearly, and listen to others; even to the dull and the ignorant; they too have their story."
Max Ehrmann, Desiderata

The gas riots of 2002 in Jamaica caused many offices to close early. Our company, however, did not issue an instruction for us to leave our post even though we were located near several hot spots connected to a volatile area. A senior member of left the office early, and this was apparently reported to the Human Resource Manager. The deputy general manager summoned me to his office a couple of days later, asking if I was the one who reported that the senior officer had left early. At that moment, my childhood flashed before me and I remembered my first experience of death. This was one Monday morning while I was at basic school. Upon arrival at my little school, we were greeted by a big crowd. A couple was shot, and there were whispers of one being shot in the mouth.

I graciously responded, *"Sir, with all due respect, I am offended that you would assume that I would report a senior officer's action, which I wasn't aware of, to the Human Resource Manager. Bear in mind, sir, that the Human Resource Manager is located at the head office. That would be out of line. Sir, where I come from in my formative years, I learned 'he that keepeth his mouth, keepeth his life.' If my abilities cannot keep me in my job, sir, I do not wish to be here. I will never, ever will be taking news to you or any other manager, sir."* He apologised that I felt that way. He explained that it was a misunderstanding as he felt disrespected as the deputy general manager that the matter was not reported to him but to the HR manager. I responded, *"Time will tell, sir. I'm here to do a job. I respect authority and, again, I would never do that."* The deputy general manager was a guest at my wedding five years later, and he became one of my greatest confidants and coach during his time at the dealership. Respect for authority is a very important trait in any organization. This can open doors of favour and also help those with whom you serve to trust to judgement and commitment to the cause.

To win in life, one needs to not only respect authority, but also respect oneself. By having respect for yourself, you will also be loyal to your convictions and cause. One day, my sales manager, BB, was rudely attacked by an expatriate, and everyone in the office was whispering and whimpering over the situation. I politely went to the new guy and asked him apologise to my manager. The manager had been a very hard worker and paved the way for him to have this experience in

Rules of the Game

Jamaica. Everyone was in shock, except my deputy general manager. He would have remembered our conversation, which I kept confidential. The new guy never apologised, and little regard was shown to him during his short stay at the dealership. In the game, it is very important for you to respect others. You show respect, earn respect, and have greater output on all levels.

To win in the workplace, we may play the game with team members who have different value systems, but we must never compromise our beliefs. I received an offer for an overseas assignment during dinner. One evening during dinner, the company's general manager informed us that he belonged to a group that some consider to be a cult. I respectfully responded, *"And I am Christian."* I wanted it to be known from the onset what my beliefs were and that those beliefs guide how I live my life in every way. It is also important to have Godly counsel, so I sought one of my spiritual leaders for his guidance. He told me that a job is no exchange, so I should accept the position and remain true to my values. The God I serve will protect me even as He provides for me. During my time on that assignment, I was careful to respect my beliefs rooted in Scripture, and I was a part of a Bible-believing community. I never partied at night but respected my vows to my Lord and family. I remained faithful to my vows as a married woman and values as Christian.

> **Game Rule #7:**
> To win in life, one needs to not only respect authority, but also respect oneself.

It is very important for us as females to be remain dignified in the professional space. Years ago, an elderly business man called Blushy told me a saying that has remained with me twenty-four years later. He said, "Never poop where you eat." While this may sound gross, this idiom is regularly used by individuals to caution others to refrain from romantic relationships in the workplace. I am truly grateful for that advice as one of the things that my deceased husband shared with me as he proposed was that I had a brand in the industry as being a professional tough lady who did kept her private life private. He said he was attracted and intrigued by this. He was not Jamaican, and he said it made him feel a sense of honour that he won the prize. He shared this story This story he shared with many who enquired about our dating and love story. Honestly, I was surprised when he mentioned it as whilst I knew it was one of my values and was very proud of my ability to have stayed focused, I thought of it as being important to me and never thought for a minute that it would impacted one of the most life altering moments in the journey of my life.

Rules of the Game

I encourage my females in the corporate game to remain ladylike. The rewards are immeasurable when you know you did not compromise to get them. Let same principle also applies to males in the workplace. Keep yourselves accountable to others and your conduct above board.

"Let love and faithfulness never leave you; bind them around your neck, write them on the tablet of your heart. Then you will win favor and a good name in the sight of God and man" (Proverbs 3: 3-4, NIV).

Throughout my journey, I have always been true to who I am. In my fortieth year, I had a new sense of strength, security, and sacredness that was exhilarating. There comes a time when our decisions collide with our destinies. I recall my work team accompanying me to my church during my ordination as a deaconess. This included my general manager and other senior managers. This moment remains one of the most fulfilling moments of my life. Our work relationships are usually significant because we spend so much time at work. You can therefore imagine my joy when my workmates validated the consistency of my values in the secular space by joining my family and I in divine worship during my ordination service. I encourage you to remain consistent with your values and your associations will be more than happy to join in your aspirations within and outside the workplace.

What then are values and how can we stay true to them in places where there are contending views? Values refer to a "person's principles or standards of behaviour." They are one's judgment of what is important in life (Oxford Languages). Identifying and understanding our principles can help us to stand firm in them. We can then respect ourselves, our beliefs, and convictions. We should demonstrate integrity and courage in both professional and personal situations in upholding our values.

As you endeavour to uphold your values, be aware that it can sometimes to be a lonely road. Be prepared, however, to stand your ground. Be prepared to gently and respectfully respond to your colleagues in moments of error as I did when an expatriate rudely attacked my sales manager. This shows loyalty and respect for those you work with. Respect is mutually constitutive and we should always seek to address situations like these with grace and dignity. This will improve our character and leadership.

As you aim to win in life, do not be afraid get wise counsel. This is important in securing your values and helping to re-centre you when you feel tempted to go against your principles. My ability to accept and work well with a leader who espouses different religious views was influenced by the advice of my confidante. Through that experience, I was able to work cohesively and this provided several opportunities for us to have dialogue and share my faith. Individuals will have different views and may even not be open to your perspective, but always be responsible in your response. Additionally, keep yourself grounded in love for humanity. This is fundamental to cooperation in the workplace. I remained committed to my faith and principles in a foreign environment, but this took a lot of strength. Like Daniel in the Bible, it is certainly possible to achieve good success without selling your soul. You can do it too!

Be consistent across your professional and personal spaces. I was confident that I could invite my work colleagues to my ordination service because I knew that they would not see a different me at church than the one that I presented at work. I encourage you to be the same person in character everywhere you so. Be consistent so that I someone should hear your name, they can speak about your character with confidently and with respect. Maintain your values, integrity, and loyalty to your causes. Continue to show respect for yourself and others as navigate life's challenges and opportunities. By staying true to your values and convictions, you maintain your self-respect and inspire others to do the same.

Coaching Tip #5: Take a few moments to think about your core values. What are some principles or standards of behaviour that are important to you? Make a list of them. How can you make sure that you never compromise on these values? Write some active statements about your values on the list and include some strategies that you will use to remain true to them. For example, "I am a truthful person. Whenever I am tempted to lie, I will still speak the truth." "I am a courteous person. When tempted to be rude, I will walk away or delay my email response until I calm down."

After you make your list of core values and strategy statements, identify some persons who you trust to give you honest, wise advice. Write down these names too. You can also group them based on the area of expertise that they have. Write some active statements about their role in your life. For example, "Whenever I need financial advice, Person A is my go-to person." "If I am confused about work-life balance, I will talk to Person B. Commit to having frequent dialogue with your advisors so that they can keep you accountable in maintaining your value system.

CHAPTER 6

SHARE THE VISION

"This above all: to thine own self be true, and it must follow, as the night the day, thou canst not then be false to any man."
William Shakespeare

"The only way you see results is if you stay consistent."
Author Unknown

Consistency

My mother's soft voice echoed loudly in my head as I found my centre in almost all my actions. Her voice of reason always calmed me and helped me to pause before I did anything I would later regret. This voice was a guiding light, reminding me to consider the feelings of others in all my actions. This emphasis on kindness and empathy became central to my identity, shaping the way I interacted with my colleagues and approached my work. When faced with decisions that would impact the lives of others, I would often ask myself, *"How would that make you feel?"* Amidst the confidence, consistency, and courage that I was practising, I was therefore also deliberate about being kind to others. I wished the best for all my work associates and did not have any evil intention toward any of them. There was a new level of gratitude in me. By this time, I was on my second stint at the first brand I represented in the heavy equipment industry. I was happy to be alive and happy to have a job where I found deep fulfilment. **What voices are you listening to?** How do these voices affect how you live out your life and do your work?

There comes a time in your life when you will receive clarity about who you are and what your purpose is. This clarity will be the impetus that you need to transform your life. In my case, I had entered a transformative period filled with newfound strength, security, and sacredness. When you enter this period, find a song that speaks to your spirit. I had Jimmy Cliff's then hit song, "The Harder They Come." The words of the chorus resonated deeply:

"So as sure as the sun will shine
I'm gonna get my share now, what's mine
And then the harder they come
The harder they fall, one and all
Ooh, the harder they come
The harder they fall, one and all."

These words served as a source of inspiration and motivation as I navigated through life's challenges in this new chapter.

As you chart a new course for our life, it is equally important to maintain a sense of humility and gratitude, never seeking to harm or mistreat others. Be also aware that you may at different points play for different teams as life, career goals and opportunities take you to different places. Do not, however, burn your bridges. Stay committed to kindness and gratitude; you will likely foster positive relationships as your colleagues learn to trust you. This, in the end, will help to contribute to a harmonious work environment as you position yourself and the team for the shift to win.

The day the Canadian expatriate expressed his confidence in my work as a consummate sales professional is one I will treasure until eternity.

"Susan, are you sitting or standing?" I was standing on the balcony of my new apartment, having moved in a little more than a year. It was a huge contrast from Trench Town, Patrick City and Hermitage. I quickly answered, *"Hello, Daniel. I am standing. It is a pleasure to hear from you."* Daniel was an expatriate who worked with the largest construction company of the day. I was relieved and happy. The last time I visited his location, the security informed me that he didn't wish to speak to anyone who worked with the company I had represented at that time, yet he tracked me down to my new place of employment.

He went on to thank me for the customer service I extended to him and applauded me for being a consummate professional; hence, his confidence in giving me an opportunity to sell him equipment. I will never forget his words, *"Whenever I make a purchase, relationship, reliability, and responsibility are the drivers in my decision process. I'm very aware that you stood up for our needs and I'm going to reward you for your efforts. I am going to buss you. Come and see me. I am requesting a quote for dozers, excavators, wheel loaders, and rollers to complete the highway."* I held on to the railings; my feet got weak, and my hands started to sweat. I stuttered. He said, *"Susan, are you there?"* For a moment, I went into what seemed like a trance. I remembered the tears I cried as I sat in my 1996 Suzuki Vitara in Half Way Tree, having learned that the position that I was in would be advertised. I left my previous job for this opportunity, and things started to get rocky. My convictions, as they relate to customer service, were not aligned with those of my new employer.

That day after receiving that news, I drove from Spanish Town Road to Tropical Plaza and cried for two hours during an extended lunchtime. Rain was falling, the sky was dark, and it was as if everything stopped moving. All I could hear was the beating of my heart and my sobs. Seeking the Lord, I prayed, *"God, You told me to take this opportunity. I sought You in prayer. King Jesus, should I remain here and fight or go back to the former company? Almighty God, I have car payments and mortgage, and if I leave this job, I will be earning one-third of what I am earning now as my basic pay."* The Holy Spirit responded with a clear, gentle voice, "Go back." The year was 2006; the date was June 16.

Daniel said, *"Susan!"* I snapped from that moment in 2006. I was crying tears of joy and relief that I was vindicated. I whispered, *"Daniel, thank you. May I please call you back?"* Listen, I yelled the biggest "Hallelujah" from the recesses of my being. The complex had 122 apartments and, to this day, some neighbours still call me "Miss Hallelujah."

By this time, I had arrears on my mortgage. I received a summons from the Supreme Court for a hearing on July 25, 2006. I was being sued by the credit union that loaned me the deposit for the apartment in excess of JA$500,000. The building society was not happy as I paid one month and skipped the other to pay the car note. Upon receiving the order for the equipment, I was therefore filled with immense relief and joy.

When I received the payment, I was careful in deploying tactics from the book *The Richest Man in Babylon*, paying tithes and saving 20% in an investment plan. Twenty years later, that plan is still active. Invest your money when there is surplus money and ensure that your investment keeps up with inflation. Wealthy people find ways to invest their money so their returns exceed inflation. Such investments are stocks, bonds, real estate, and life insurance policies which have an investment component.

> **Game Rule #8:**
> Invest your money whenever there is a surplus and ensure that your investment keeps up with inflation.

Favour the Faithful

The company I returned to won the deal from the larger equipment supplier. It was my second tenure there and I was the sales rep who won the deal and enabled them to receive the largest order for the year from that deal. The night before payday, I got a vision. I saw a group of ladies, including myself, and we were making beds in what seemed like a classroom. However, the building was a bar across the road from the church I attended. The Holy Spirit then instructed me to give JA$30,000 as an offering to church, separate from my tithes. I started to wail in the morning, *"Lord, You know I have all these outstanding expenses, yet I say yes. Yes, Lord."* I took the envelope to my pastor that very evening and gave him the envelope with the offering. I held the summons for the outstanding amount and said, *"Rev, accept this sacrificial offering. Accept it, and do not block what the Lord has in store."* I continued, *"Although I have the summons, I have said yes"* and I shared the vision about making the beds. I was sweating; Rev prayed with me and accepted the offering.

Rules of the Game

I remember as clear as day when he said, *"God shall open the windows of heaven and pour you out a blessing that you have no room to store it."* Indeed, God was faithful to His promise. Within two months after receiving the vision, I earned over one million Jamaican dollars. To this day, I have the cheque receipt as a testament of the faithfulness of God.

Jeremiah 29:11 says, *"For I know the plans I have for you declares the Lord, plans to prosper and not to harm you, plans to give you hope and a future"* (NIV). The children of Israel, in the period of the writings of Jeremiah 29, were banished to the rulership of the Babylonians. Yet, the Lord promised them that nothing would harm them. He also promised them that they would be blessed in those years as they continued to pray for the city where they were living. I bought a house in faith on a measly salary, having left a secure position with higher renumeration. I trusted the process and believed that nothing would harm me. It was therefore sheer agony and humiliation when I needed to return to my former place of employment. Things were not working out at the new company, yet God remained faithful. Today, whenever I see that Scripture, I personalise it. I believe it and confess it. **Whatever your season, situation or station, hold firm to the belief that it is well!**

That sale became the catalyst of my career. My name echoed throughout the industry; a small axe cut down a big tree by winning the deal from a significantly larger brand and cemented the brand I was representing at that time on the map of Jamaica. Parallel to the construction boom in

Jamaica in 2006–2009, our company's sales boomed. In another two years, we also won another significant deal with a bauxite company, outbidding the competition yet another time.

I was intrigued with sales, having received training from the renowned R. Danny Williams, who pointed out that for every five calls, there should be a close. I planned my daily calls, executed and closed. Our team was a three-member band, and I was very mindful of how critical it was in supporting my team at all costs. My head was buried in my work; I was enjoying the challenges and, at that time, we had a construction boom from several Spanish hotels and other developments that were taking place across the island.

The company employed additional team members. I heartily shared information and assisted the new commercial manager at the time. The department was now split in two, so I was assisting as a sales rep in both divisions. Time went by so fast. I didn't realize that the new guy had decided to leave; however, what he did was both admirable and life-changing. He remained true to himself and his passions. I asked him why he was leaving and he shared that he was not fascinated by the industry; his heart wasn't in it. He was more interested in the Financial Industry and recommended that they promote me to be the Commercial Division Manager. The promotion to Commercial Manager did not come with any fanfare or support staff, but I was elated to be one of the quarterbacks on the team. Finally I was off the bench and playing in a leading role. I was promoted and my salary was doubled. I also got a company car. I was overjoyed; things were working out. I also recognised an opportunity to expand our offerings by suggesting that we deliver our batteries. This is how ASK Couriers, my family business was birthed as I was given the contract to deliver the same. Indeed, the Lord used these moments and others to bless my efforts and to confirm His word to me that He had instructed me to return to my former place of employment.

Colossians 3:23 says, *"Whatever you do, work at it with all your heart as working for the Lord, not for human masters"* (NIV). This scripture became my mantra. My head was down, busily doing the next thing. I did not even realize that God has sent my "Deliverer" as Delroy, a then new recruit at the company, upon leaving, recommended that I should be promoted. Today he is serving as a Vice President at one of Jamaica's leading financial institutions. I have been careful to pay it forward by recognising and rewarding talents where it is possible just as Delroy did for me. Thank you, "Moses."

I saw God directing my steps in another incident. The company was undergoing some major changes, including having an overseas consultant to assist with remodelling its organisational and physical infrastructure. Little did I know that the company was in negotiations to be sold. During that same time, I received another vision. I saw new owners, the staff dressed in black and white, and the Holy Spirit shared with me that the consultant would be returning to the United

Kingdom. Exactly as it appeared in the vision, the company was sold and the uniform of the new owners was black and white.

Concurrently, there were advanced talks of my church owning the building across the street that I had had a previous vision about. My confidence soared with the leading of the Holy Spirit. I had faith that my steps were ordered according to His Word. In fact, today, the bar is now our church's cook shop. Another section of the building is utilised as the church's basic school and also hosts our adult Sunday School.

I shared the vision of the new owners with some co-workers, and in private, I shared the word with the parts consultant that he would be returning home soon. (After my encounter with the bidding of the Holy Spirit to give the offering, the experience of a victory in the closing of the deal, and the turnaround in my finances, I was encouraged to share when the Lord directed me to speak). I will never forget his words; *"You are so correct, Susan. I will be leaving the company soon, and there is no way you could have known. Continue being a very good sales rep; always remember, be a tall dog and never pee like a puppy."* I asked him what he meant by that, and he explained that we work in a patriarchal environment. Men have the liberty to release themselves anywhere, but a lady cannot do that. He said, *"Never come down to our level as a means of being accepted in the club. Keep your dignity. Do not be kiss up, but demand and accept the chivalry of men."*

Keeping Scores

"Creativity is seeing what others see and thinking what no one else ever thought." —Albert Einstein

Every competitive game keeps scores so that a winner can be declared at the end. The winner, of course, can only win if they follow the rules of the game. When watching a game in person or on television, we pay attention to the scores at the end of each quarter, at half-time, and especially at the end. For players in the game, watching the scores let them know whether they are behind or ahead, how much work they need to put it, and whether they need to change or maintain their game strategies. The creative coach will use the same score line that everyone sees, but come up with unique strategies to keep the team composed and advance to victory. Keeping scores is therefore very important.

My scorecard shows that I spent twenty years in the heavy equipment industry where I did two stints at two major companies in the industry: Company A (2001-2004), Company B (2004-2006), Company A (2006-2011), and Company B (2011-2020). Upon leaving Company B in 2006, during my exit interview, I shared an email with the HR and sales managers, requesting that I be considered for an opportunity to sell after-sales parts and services. The position would be an opportunity for personal growth, and the company would also benefit from my experience selling equipment for the competing brand, in addition to the equipment that the company represented. Unfortunately, the position was not available then, and furthermore, the Lord instructed me to return to Company A, so if the position had been offered then, I would not have taken it. The instructions were clear: "Leave that position and return to your former position."

Unbeknownst to me, God had a plan. In 2011, I sensed that I should resign for a second time, having returned there in to Company A in 2006. I was having challenges finishing my undergraduate studies and my husband was in a very good job, so I sensed an opportunity, after twenty-two years of working, to be a stay-at-home mom. I was happy and ready to submit my resignation letter, when I received a call to apply for a job opening at Company B. I was like, "Lord, I refuse to return to the hardship that I endured in that place." Nonetheless, I went through the recruitment process and accepted the Department Manager position. This was the same position which I had suggested in 2006 when I was serving as a sales clerk. I wrote the vision, and though it tarried, it came to pass. I was now a senior manager at the same company I had to retreat from years ago with no bitterness in my heart. I was now sitting at that table with my former boss as a "tall dog" without having to compromise. My heart was filled with love and gratitude. Creativity was critical in this segment of play, and the confidence in my abilities was my anchor.

My belief in my capacity and dreams were inviolable. I had a new approach to ministry and secular work. This was cemented as I was voted to serve in a leadership capacity at my local church. I was not a theologian, neither did I go up through the ranks of the church. In the grand scheme of things, I was a young convert, yet I was nominated to serve on the church board as a Deaconess. Our Senior Pastor expressed to me that he knew it was supernatural for me to be a member of the board. His words were to me were, "Having you at this table, I know it is the only the work of the Lord." Psalm 37:23 says that, "the steps of good man are ordered by the Lord and he delighteth in his way" (KJV). I will always remember and be buoyed by this Scripture.

The realisation that the purpose of man is to serve and do the master's will had become the catalyst for all that I did after my conversion to a dedicated Christian life. I became conscious of the words written in Micah 6:8, *"He has shown you, O man, what is good; and what does the Lord require of you but to do justly, to love mercy, and to walk humbly with your God?"* (NKJV). My opportunity to serve as a deaconess in my community church was and is my most fulfilling assignment. Fulfilling my purpose gives me the assurance that I am living a victorious life.

Keeping scores is very important in the game. As you serve and give when challenges arise, call to mind your past victories. It is important to record your statistics, wins, losses, deals closed, and growth percentages. Your scorecard helps to tell your story. Be prepared to tell that story often. You are a winner in the game of life. You always get back up from every loss. You are a winner because you never stop fighting. *"Winner's win."*

I have recorded so many triumphs as I moved forward with faith and fearlessness. Every test that I faced was the springboard to activate my faith and draw on my inner fortitude. Recognizing and celebrating your successes can serve as a source of motivation and allow you to reflect on God's faithfulness and guidance in your life. Embrace your challenges and use them as opportunities to activate your faith and draw on your inner strength. You will find that you have more resilience and determination than you think. As you continue to move forward even in the face of adversity, you demonstrate your trust in the fact that there is a bigger and better plan for your life. Keeping score and acknowledging help or set plays in the game denotes positivity, humility, and perseverance. Your scorecard will show you how far you have come and give you hope for the future. It shows you what it possible as you move forward in your purpose with vivacious creativity and tenacity.

Power in Proclamation

As I accepted the position to serve as a board member at the church in the community where I grew up as a teenage mother, I remembered the conversation with the HR manager at my first permanent job in government when I applied for maternity leave in my third trimester. I was advised at that moment that, unfortunately, I did not qualify for maternity leave as I needed to be employed for a year, and that the only leave I was entitled to was six weeks. I was also scoffed at by the HR manager. She stated that I should be submitting additional subjects and not a request for maternity leave. As I responded to her, I remembered a sweet, elderly, well-spoken community member called Mrs. Consie. She always reminded me that it is important to think before speaking. *"Words cannot be taken back or eaten,"* she would say. She would share tales of persons saying or doing unkind things to her, yet she remained dignified. In that moment, I remembered Mrs Consie. and the stories that she shared of beratement and loss yet she always ensured that her words were seasoned with grace. In my best Mrs. Consie's. voice, I responded, *"With all due respect, while I understand your disappointment that I am a teenage mother, I promise you I will make the best of this opportunity. Remember my name; mark this name: Susan Gordon. I will make something of my life. Your words today are a motivation to do well, and by God's grace, I will."*

I went on to do well at the government agency where I spent three and half years, consistently copping special incentives and being placed on special projects. As I transitioned into insurance, the government agency became my feeder for prospects, and the said HR manager gave me a lead to her family, and I was always met with a warm smile. I went on to receive a "Rookie" award at my branch and became a consistent Century Club member. I was never one to make excuses as a seventeen-year-old teenage mother, or a single mother with two young children, or an expatriate on an overseas assignment with an ailing husband. I was persuaded that my steps were ordered, and that I was created to serve. My experiences are a fulfilment of purpose. Every encounter is a part of the process to fulfil the promises of God. I was called to serve on my local church board only eight years after my conversion. In the same way, I worked hard in secular, so did I within the sacred walls of the church. I was ready to serve with grace, patience, and confidence. I believed in the power of abundance and knew that I was walking in a season of Ephesians 3:20: *"Now to Him who is able to do exceedingly abundantly above all that we ask or think, according to the power that works in us"* (NKJV). There is power in the spoken word. I spoke into my destiny and I never looked back. **Life is what you make it**!

Coaching Tip #6: Take a few moments to think about your life's scorecard. What are your statistics? Do you have more triumphs than losses or vice versa? What do you think accounts for how you are doing in the game? What strategies can you come up with to improve your game plan? Write them down and commit to following them.

As you reflect on your scorecard, recognize that the stage that you are at in your life may require you to change teams by working with a different company in your industry, or leaving that industry altogether. Be honest with yourself. Is the industry you are in where your heart really is? If you are studying, is your course of study positioning you for what you really want to do in life? If you are retired or unemployed, are you engaging in activities that daily fill you with joy and purpose? If your scorecard shows that you are not where you are being most fulfilled, be like Delroy and take the bold step away from where you are and into where you really want to be.

Look around you. Is there someone in your community or workplace that you can recommend for a promotion or an award? If so, mention their name(s) to the relevant persons so that they can be appropriately recognized or promoted.

Finally, visit your scorecard frequently. Adjust as is necessary. The game is never over until the final whistle.

CHAPTER 7

RESTORATION

"I'm convinced that about half of what separates the successful entrepreneur from the non-successful ones is pure perseverance."
Steve Jobs

Shooting of Target

It was in Peoria, Illinois in 2017 that I received clear instructions in a vision to stick to the plan. I was on my sixth trip to my then company's factory as a participant in a dealer exchange training. I recall sharing the instructions with my daughter, Mother Chloe, and prayer partners. It is very important to have accountable partners throughout your journey. The instructions had five clear steps. These included: an increase in reading the Word of God, be the best wife and mother, do a public speaking course, advancing Deborah N. O.W. ministry (a non-profit organisation that I founded. The acronym stands for Nurturing Our Women), and to shoot for the stars.

I went into motion. By February 2018, I was enrolled in one of Jamaica's best public speaking courses with Adrian Atkinson as our facilitator. The day after I registered, I was traveling to another country to share my best practices and to facilitate a sales training. In March 2018, Deborah N.O.W was recognised in the Jamaican Gleaner for our intervention in a high school that was experiencing challenges with high teenage pregnancy. My husband also needed my support, having suffered a heart attack that thwarted his plans to return to his homeland, Australia. Heeding the call to be the best wife in that season, I stood by him.

My place of employment was also doing exceptionally well, and we had record sales in 2017. Restoration was the order of the day. As an individual, I received my most fulfilling appraisal and, of course, financial gains. My husband was in the hospital but I was also able to host a customer seminar at work. No excuses, no prisoners. "It is what it is," became my mantra.

I continued to serve passionately during this time because I was determined to honour my commitments to all. I remembered the commitments that I had made during my job interview and I made up my mind that I would never destroy that trust. Over time I had therefore earned the respect of my colleagues and the statistics were also there to show that we were doing well.

Hence, even when the family challenges came, and rest assured, they will come—life is life—I needed to travel to

Australia in the first quarter, and the trust was garnered to allow me to travel that distance for ten days. Although I had planned for ten days, the trip had to be extended for five more days due to challenges with my frail, ailing husband. Things did not go as smoothly as we had planned, so we decided it would be better to return to Jamaica. In that moment, I remembered my plan to be the best wife and mother. I also saw in my husband, his determination to be the best husband and family member as he tried to reconnect with his roots. We embraced, and I explained to him with a sob, *"I'm on a journey, all of us, and I understand your decision and will not abandon my husband here and embarrass my convictions and the name of Jesus Christ. I will take you home and care for you until the Lord says it is over."* As I spoke, I was trembling. I did not have a ticket for him to return, and the cost of travel between Jamaica and Australia is huge. Hence, I reached out to my base in the USA, and they heartily agreed to host him for a period as he was always so kind and compassionate. This was more affordable for me, and he recuperated there satisfactorily. **All's well that ends well**.

Kinnane was a hardworking and witty person with a good sense of humour. He was also a great provider and protector for his family and friends. He made our island his home and was super loyal to the extent that members of the major political parties used to jokingly tease him that he had also become a supporter of his wife's political party. His words were few yet strong. In December 2019, when he passed away, his son's tribute was a testament to the man and the life that he lived. I will always cherish the words of Junior Kinnane: *"Dad would always let us feel safe and confident; it doesn't matter the day we had. Our home was safe because dad made it safe."* Life is a journey and sometime some things come full circle. My husband never met my father, but they had so much in common. My father was an astute business man and so was my husband. My father did everything he could to provide and keep us safe and so did my husband. My father would have been proud as I understood the assignment in choosing a life partner.

My journey in shooting for the stars is filled with divine guidance and personal growth moments. I knew that I could never settle for mediocrity. The clear instructions that I received in a vision while on that trip served as a roadmap for my action and acted as a guide toward my goals and aspirations. It is the path of confidence and courage and I am committed to following it despite the challenges.

By increasing my focus on reading the Word of God and prioritizing my roles as a wife and mother, I established a strong foundation for personal and spiritual growth. During the challenging time of my husband's illness, I stuck to shooting the target and stayed committed to being the best wife by providing him with unwavering support and standing by his side. It was tough, but I understood the importance of prioritizing family and relationships amidst personal and professional pursuits.

I cannot overemphasize how much I drew from my spiritual foundation and the support of family and friends during those days. This foundation helped me to keep my priorities in line and kept my mind and heart steady when things got overwhelming. Aligning your actions with divine guidance and support from loved ones will enable you to experience significant strides even in difficult times.

I am a life-long learner, so enrolling in the public speaking course and advancing Deborah N.O.W. helped me to continue to make inroads in my quest towards self-improvement and community engagement. You too can be impactful and continuously improve if you work on the fundamental things in your life.

Winning the game and encouraging team members to stay committed to the task requires effective communication. The public speaking course was therefore an important investment in honing my communication skills. I learned how to organize my thoughts, how to make speeches more memorable, and also how to read audiences. I used these skills right away when I travelled overseas to conduct a sales training. How would you rate your public speaking abilities? What can you do to improve yourself in this area? Courses and speaking opportunities can help you to improve in this area.

> **Game Rule #9:**
> Effective communication skills are needed to win in life. Invest in a public speaking course or other training opportunities to improve how you communicate.

Despite the odds, I experienced restoration. I went through the fire but came out like pure gold (Job 23:10). Previously, I felt like every encounter was an interrogation where I had to defend myself and my actions. Now, I see them as an opportunity to learn, share my thoughts with others and develop mutual understanding. I seek for ways in which I can be of benefit to others and to not take myself so seriously. I feel free. Free to be myself and to walk in my purpose. A part of that purpose is to help others. Martin Luther King Jr. once echoed the following words that are immortalized in song: *"If you can help somebody along the way, then your living is not in vain."* I have been so deliberate in looking for opportunities to do good that I have a mural on my kitchen counter to remind me of this truth.

In my season of restoration, Deborah N.O.W. parachuted to another level. We joined efforts with our international partners, Empowered Women International and what a collaboration it was! Dr. Alicia Louis-Potter and her team joined our local team, and we journeyed to the rural high school that faced the challenges of high teenage pregnancy. The team journeyed on some treacherous roads, but we persisted because we believed it to be a worthy cause. The first visit was a fact-finding mission followed by the intervention session. We tried to get an understanding of the dynamics of the situation and the many factors that could have led to it. It was after this that we imparted some intervention strategies. We are forever grateful to the late Dr. Chloe Morris, a founding member and Social Director of Deborah N.O.W., who guided us skilfully on during the process. Thank you, Bro. Morris and family, for selflessly sharing Dr. Chloe with us. Deborah N.O.W. and those girls are better because she gave. We are so grateful that we got the opportunity to honour her as Woman of the Year in 2019 when we celebrated seven years of the movement. My mother, Beverly, would often remind us, **"Give the roses now."**

Deborah N.O.W. Ministry has also been blessed by the support of our chairman, Bishop Paul Morris his faithful wife, Rev. Sandra Morris, who together led the team of evangelists on this mission. Over ten individuals from different denominations also supported us by responding to the clarion call. Kudos to my own coach and editor of this book, Crystal Daye, who took the journey with us and supported the vision. Today she is the springboard into my destiny as a published author. I am the same girl who a university professor declared as dyslexic and a dunce. Stay on course, my friend, and remain clear with the vision that

God has placed in your heart. Clarity can bring you one step closer to making your dream a reality.

I serve as Founder and President of Deborah N.O.W. Ministry, but I keep our plans submitted to the leadership of the church where I serve. My former pastor and his wife, Rev. Dr. Stevenson and Larene Samuels therefore also played a role in helping us meet our objectives. They asked for an outline of our plans as we embarked on that mission. Thank you, Sister Larene and Dr. Sam for your guidance. The strategy was deployed successfully as there was an alignment on all levels with all the stakeholders involved. In fact, that same year, the theme for my place of employment was "Alignment" and I came to appreciate how God had orchestrated that moment to fulfil His purpose.

Our response to the issues at that high school was a Girls' Day, where we hosted over three hundred girls and their parents. The following year, we donated a stove and launched a Boys' Day initiative. Shooting the target, our intervention plans aimed to build awareness of the rights of children, improving parenting skills and interpersonal development. We were focused on dealing with the issues head-on so that our children can live fulfilled lives. We were effective warriors as the game was won. *"Like arrows in the hand of a warrior, so are the children of one's youth"* (Psalms 127:4 – NKJV). To date, that school has not experience a repeat of those challenges. We did it without an ulterior motive; we simply responded to the call. I responded because I am a surviving teenage mother. Due to a successful support system, I made it through, and I believed in my story enough to share. I believed in my story enough to know that those young girls could also overcome. Deborah N.O.W., by this time, had built the credits to call the nation to do more to protect our children. We were featured and honoured in the Jamaican Flair, March 2018 edition in recognition of our work in the social enhancement space. This, however, was not an isolated incident as from 2013 we had involved a cadre of counsellors, nurses, and lawyers to give legal advice, health management tips and psycho-social tips. We have also provided numerous scholarships, financial support and care packages to persons who are facing dire circumstances. Deborah N.O.W. has grown because we wrote the vision, and though it tarried, it came through at an appointed time.

Restoration reigned in that season. Our company's customer seminar that year was held at a prominent hotel, and I was asked to be the mistress of ceremony. By then, I had honed my public speaking skills, and the reviews were astounding. Coach Adrian was as proud as a peacock when I shared snippets of my deliberations. Incidentally, it was CC, one of my spiritual daughters, who encouraged me to participate in the course. I have been careful to encourage others to also participate in this course and have also sponsored some of them. This is my way of paying forward because I have seen what it has done for me and want others to also experience this growth and confidence in their public speaking skills. As you participate and grow from opportunities, do the same by paying it forward.

Forgiveness Precedes Restoration

Finally, in the plan to shoot for the stars was a desire for a business. I wanted to do something new. There was limited opportunity for growth in my present employment, yet I volunteered on projects and initiated some. I started incentive programs for customers and staff and this resulted in a greater staff engagement team. We had programs that were designed for leaders to visit a factory, and we were able to help two members get an opportunity to visit the factory in Peoria, Illinois. Other senior members were given opportunities for training at the corporate office and other dealer exchange programs in the United States. By the end of 2018, 71% of the senior sales team received dealer onsite training, and the support team received incentives due to improved sales for the products that we pushed and exceeded targets. Another major achievement in that season of restoration was that the dealership received recognition for online sales in Latin America. A now middle-aged teenage mother, who completed her first degree at forty-two years old, shot for the stars and broke the glass ceiling.

An opening also came for an overseas assignment, which provided an opportunity to learn other skills and share my experience of almost nineteen years in the game. The assignment was short-lived due to the effects of COVID-19, but it provided the greatest restoration of all: forgiveness. I grieved and released the loss of that opportunity and forgave myself for thinking my departure was untimely. Our steps are ordered and even the very things that seem to be missteps are a part of the process. I also had the humility to seek forgiveness from my then employer. Based on where we were, it seemed like I had rocked the boat. It was very important to forgive myself and to also seek forgiveness. The unforgiveness was like a great stone tied to my back; it was a crushing weight that I carried everywhere I went. It was even more difficult to let go of because the offender was myself.

During it all, one of my deepest desires was fulfilled, which was to restart ASK Couriers. Having left Company A a second time and taken up the managerial position at Company B, it would have been a conflict of interest to be delivering batteries for company A. Hence, I decided to cease operations and focus on my full-time employment at Company B. My children were very disheartened as they were looking forward to being involved in the business as they got older. I assured them that, "what is for you, is for you." Restoration did come as this same company, Company B, gave me an exclusive contract in the middle of the COVID-19 pandemic to deliver parts to their customers island wide. Now, if this is not what restoration looks like, I don't know what else is! This was professionalism, grace and kindness at their highest. I got a second chance to restore the trust that the company had vested in me and served diligently and indefatigably as a delivery girl. I represented the company, delivering millions of products and responding to calls 24/7. The feedback was superb and I will forever cherish the opportunity for ASK Couriers to be rebirthed.

Shooting for the target requires an attitude like that of one of the world's greatest leaders, Sir Winston Churchill: *Never give up! Never give up! Never give up!* Like a tree planted by the rivers of waters, stick to your inherent plans, and whatever you do, you will prosper and experience restoration. I mention inherent because it is my belief that what you do to experience the restoration is likely very personal and you have the tools within you to make it possible.

Coaching Tip #7: Unforgiveness is a heavy burden that blocks your progress and that of others. Take some time to think about any incident in the workplace or in your other interpersonal relationships where you blame yourself for the outcome. Take responsibility for your role in the outcome by admitting that there are things that you could have done differently. Acknowledge the fact that as humans, we are imperfect beings and therefore make mistakes. Write a note to yourself by admitting where you went wrong and forgive yourself. For example, "The day I had the argument with employee X, I was angry and said things that I should not have said. I am sorry for the strained relationship that we now have. I grieve the loss of friendship and forgive myself for the unkind words that I said." Read your note aloud and then burn the paper. Each time that you remember what happened, say out loud, "I forgive myself and I have moved on."

After you release yourself, try to identify persons you may have unintentionally or even intentionally hurt and seek for opportunities to apologize. This may be an evening after work, seeing each other in the restroom, or just asking the person when might be a good time to have a conversation. Be humble in your apology and do not try to blame the other person. As you prepare to apologize, recognize that the person may or may not accept your apology and that the apology may not always lead to the relationship being restored to its former state. As much as it depends on you, however, your apology can clear the air and help to restore at minimum, civility and respect in your interactions with others. Forgive yourself, ask for forgiveness and be also open to forgiving others.

CHAPTER 8

WIN: THE PEAK

"Discipline is choosing between what you want now and what you want most."
Abraham Lincoln

Discipline will determine the win. Throughout this book, you would have observed one constant: discipline, discipline, and discipline—the discipline to complete what was started and the remain focused throughout. Discipline requires trusting the process and involving others to fulfil their purpose. This will result in the village's growth so no one will be left behind in enjoying the spoils of the victory. That is what winning looks like. This requires thinking big, setting smart goals, and effectively mobilizing resources. As the African proverb indicate, *"If you want to go fast, go alone. If you want to go far, go together."*

Having returned to Jamaica due to COVID, I found myself without a job, husband, or company car, yet the economic demands surrounded me like a tree. The income from ASK

Couriers was insufficient, so I sought employment. Seven months and nine interviews later, I believed that my present employer was the one. In the chapter on faith, it is stated that faith precedes favor, adding that faith must be a discipline. Prayer and believing in the word of God concerning your situation are essential. After my first interview with the food distribution giant, I decided to exercise my faith, believing I would be driving to work on Harbour Street. I extended my faith by scheduling a photo shoot at the Kingston Waterfront and Harbour Street, near my desired employer.

Interestingly, there was an expansion project at the waterfront, and the equipment on site belonged to one of the first companies where I sold a backhoe loader in 2001. We proceeded with the first shooting on the site, and fortunately, my photographer Hanifa caught the vision and agreed with me.

Despite no longer being employed in the heavy equipment industry, I took photographs in the element, just like in the past when I visited sites as a heavy equipment sales rep. My spirit was ignited with joy as we did the photo shoot on the construction site, looking onward to the company logo positioned on top of a crown. I received a spiritual confirmation that day that I would receive employment at the company and ended the photo shoot by walking on Harbour Street, declaring, "The earth is the Lord's and its fullness thereof. Like Joshua, wherever my feet trod belongs to me." Unbeknownst to Hanifa, who didn't know I had done the interview, she joined me in prayer and caught the vision.

Today, I am employed by the food distribution giant, with the company office located on Harbour Street, and what a journey it has been.

Notably, I had the privilege of celebrating 100 years as a member of the team and am an elated owner of stocks in the company, which were gifted to employees as the company celebrated its 100th anniversary. What are the odds that I would join the company in its 99th year and benefit from that glorious season of celebration?

As you read this book, your desires will likely be activated. Be disciplined to have faith, believing that you will experience the joy of answered prayers. Dress up and show up. Start preaching to trees or teaching Sunday School; it might require that you start with your siblings. Single ladies, buy that wedding dress, and to the man who desires a new car, visit that dealership and test drive the car. Discipline and faith are a winning combination. Holding onto faith and being disciplined in taking positive steps can lead to unexpected and rewarding outcomes.

Winning also requires you to be honest with yourself about your capabilities and rising to the occasion when the opportunity arises. I joined a new team at another company in the height of COVID-19. In this new company, Company C, I experienced the joy of an overflowing cup. My responsibilities included managing a team and a fleet of trucks. My relationship with this company goes as far back as twenty years ago, where while at one of my previous places of employment, I was assigned to the account as a vehicle sales representative. Today, units that I sold are in the present fleet of this company. I consider this a winning moment because I am able to see how previous work linked two companies and enabled me to be a beneficiary today. My passion for the units, years of experience in aftermarket products, and skills in social work and sales all formed an axis around which I have been able to make an impact in the world of work. These skills coupled with my faith, have become my winning strategy. Winning will require you to courageously embark into unknown territories, stay true to your convictions, and be confident in your capabilities, even when the landscape of the game changes. These are the rules of the game.

What are the odds that a gentleman would give me a career-defining advice: *"Susan, you need to ask the customers, 'Why?' In understanding the why, you will be able to define what is the solution."* These words helped to carve a career path for me, leading me into a leadership position at a company where that same person had served as Group CEO. In all the steps that I have made, I have always bered to seek customer input so that we can better meet their needs. Being consistent in discovering the "Why" at all levels where you serve will also be critical for you as you too seek continued growth and good success.

While still learning, it is safe to say that I am no longer parked on the bench or stagnated as the quarterback who has seen better days. Instead, I am at the peak of success where

I am a valuable and committed member of the team with the proven statistics to solidify our wins. I am in a season where we are reaping the proceeds of the process. Seasons change, but there are always opportunities to win. Stick to the plan and in due season, you too will experience your peak.

As you reach the peak of success, always make sure to take someone along with you and advocate on their behalf. When my administrative assistant was made redundant thirteen years ago, I confidently presented a business proposal to justify why the business needed her. She returned to her position and went on to an established career, being a viable talent in the company, leading various projects and receiving employee recognition repeatedly. A timid inside sales representative asked me about my thoughts on her accepting a position for field sales representative. I took her on an on-the-job experience at a customer event where she observed me engaging customers, having meaningful conversations, and establishing relationships. The following Monday, I explained to her that having meaningful relationships is important in sales and something that she could also learn. Using what was modelled at the customer event, I encouraged her that she too had the gift, grace, and personality to do the same and more. Ten years later, she established herself in the game and became an expert in the industry. At one point, she was based out of town. Winning is sweeter when you achieve success not only in your personal endeavours, but also when you see others who you have mentored also winning in their lives.

Every winning team has a playmaker. In games such as football, this is "the person who leads the attack, or brings other players on the same side into a position from which they could score" (Oxford Languages). As you track your many wins in life, the scorecard will help you identify moments when you have been a playmaker by leading the attack on your team, or positioning others to score so that the team can win. The playmaker is therefore important in positioning and coordinating game strategies within the organizations. As I reflect on my two previous work assignments, I see instances where I was positioned to play well by a playmaker, and also times where I was the playmaker. I can identify key customer management positions that were recommended in my business strategy and which continue to be pivotal in the growth of those companies. Our strategies should be sustainable, so that even after we have moved or retired from our positions, the work that we put in place will still be actioned and withstand the test of time.

> **Game Rule #10:**
> Every winning team has a playmaker. There will be times when you will play this role by leading the attack or positioning others on the team to score.

A playmaker believes and persists in order to win the game. Jack Canfield said this: *"Persistence is probably the single most common quality of high achievers. They simply refuse to give up."* Refuse to give up in the game of life. The longer you hang in there, the greater the chance that something will happen in your favour. No matter how hard it seems, the longer you persist, the more likely your success will be.

Dogged determination determines the win. If you suffer loss, yet believe in your ability to regain, like an eagle you will rise above the status quo. B.C. Forbes, the founder of Forbes magazine, once stated, *"History has demonstrated the most notable winners usually encountered heart-breaking obstacles before they triumphed. They won because they refused to become discouraged by their defeats."* There has never been a successful person who has never known failure or has not overcome staggering odds. Refuse to become discouraged by your defeats. I share below some examples of some winners in the game. They suffered many defeats, but they refused to be discouraged or defeated by them.

    a. Thomas Edison —His grade school teachers said he was *"Too stupid to learn anything."* Yet he helped develop many inventions that ushered in the modern age. These include the motion picture camera, the phonograph, and a practical light bulb. Edison was also an extraordinary businessman who was an early advocate of mass production and teamwork in the process of innovation, with over 1,000 US patents (Logan, 2022). Do not be discouraged by the voices of authority in your life which may have called you stupid or think you were unfit for a particular career path. You can rise above those odds to become a gamechanger in your field.

b. **Abraham Lincoln** —Lincoln had his share of setbacks, including failing in business, failing to get into law school and suffering from depression. He was also defeated for nomination to the U.S. Congress and defeated again for nomination for Vice President. He continually kept moving forward, and was elected President of the United States in 1860 (Weltman, 2021). Keep your focus on your goals. You may be defeated for an opportunity, but your spirit does not have to be defeated. Remain undaunted by the challenges that you face and keep forward. One day, this determination will propel you beyond your wildest dreams.

c. **Akio Morita** —His first company was called Tokyo Telecommunications Engineering Corp, which was formed after a failed attempt to market a rice cooker that either burnt the rice or didn't cook it properly. Rather than making knock-off products like many other companies of his day, Morita wanted to develop quality innovative companies, and focused on a pocket-size radio. The best he could develop was just a bit too large for a typical pocket, so he had his salesmen wear shirts with oversized pockets so the radio would fit. This radio became a hit. Morita also foresaw the importance of branding, and changed the name of his company to Sony (GSMArena, 2015). Today, the Sony brand is very well known. Do not give up if your first business attempt flops. Take the time to consider other products and services that the market needs. Be patient. Your next business idea may just be what you become known for.

d. **Elon Musk** —Musk poured all of his $200 million pay-out from PayPal into his next two companies – SpaceX and then Tesla Motors. At one point, while tethering on the verge of bankruptcy, Musk debated if he should get rid of one of his companies so the other would succeed. He stuck with both, and the companies slowly made progress (through continual uphill battles). Musk and his team have accomplished the seemingly impossible, as both companies are revolutionizing their respective industries. Musk's net worth is estimated by Forbes to be over USD 200 billion (Forbes 2024; Wealthpreneur, 2023). Winning in life can sometimes mean trudging through losses for a period of time. While it may sometimes be prudent to cut unprofitable ventures and focus on those that have the potential to be profitable, there are other times when the losses are only seasonal. Make sure that you understand the industry that you work in so that you can distinguish between those things that are temporary and those that are more permanent.

e. **Elvis Presley** —The king hardly needs an introduction. Yet when Presley tried out as a vocalist for the Eddie Bond band, Bond rejected him with the advice to stick to driving *"because you're never going to make it as a singer"* (Yardley, 2013). Similarly, Presley was told by Jim Denny, the manager of the Grand Ole Opry, *"You ain't going nowhere, son; you ought to be back to driving a truck"* (Simpson, 2020). Know yourself and the gifts that you possess. Be willing to identify as well, those people who should be a part of your story and those who shouldn't be. Elvis Presley's story was written by people who recognized his talents and helped him soar to his destiny. Not everyone will recognize your value and that is ok. It just means that they were never meant to be a main character in the story of your life.

f. **Oprah Winfrey** —Born in an economically troubled neighbourhood and raised by a single teenage mom, Oprah experienced considerable hardship, including being physically abused as a teenager. Today, Winfrey is a renowned media proprietor, talk show host, actress, and philanthropist. Her net worth is approximately USD 3 billion (The Kennedy Center, 2024; Martin, 2024). Where you start does not have to be where you end. Be willing to rise above the challenges of your beginnings to craft the endings that you desire. The path before you may not be easy, but it is possible if you plan and persist towards it.

Rules of the Game

In conclusion, there are many examples of people across the world who achieved success after many failures. Despite the odds, they remained undaunted in the game of life. You too can experience good success if you remain steadfast and not derelict your duties. Remain disciplined and dogged with determination as you uphold your convictions. Remember that adherence to the rules of the game in this book will be a springboard for you to have good success and prevent you from selling your soul. Never shy away from the process. **Process** is the conduit to ignite your **purpose** and walk into your **promise.** Stay focused and run the race that is set before you.

As you begin to reflect on your own game and the strategies that you want to use to win, I leave with you **Ten Key Principles** that will help you experience good success without selling your soul.

1. **Desire Righteousness In All Your Ways** — *"Blessed are those who hunger and thirst for righteousness, for they shall be filled"* (NIV). Righteousness refers to doing what is morally right. It is about being virtuous in one's actions. God will honour your desires. If you therefore desire to do what is right at all times then God will enable you to live off that desire wherever you go. Prayerfully seek Him for guidance and He will give clarity on what your desires should be (see Proverbs 3:3-6).

2. **Dream and Write the Vision** —A dream is a general goal while a vision involves concrete steps to make that goal reality. Your dream will therefore require a personal vision. In some cases, you may be able to singlehandedly accomplish your dream, but in other instances, you may need the support of others. Be bold and share your dream with others. Be clear and specific with your vision. There is power in a clear and well-written vision. Write your goals on a piece of paper or type them on the computer or on your phone. Put concrete steps and timelines beside these goals and be intentional about achieving them.

3. **Discipline** — Discipline requires doing the hard and sometimes mundane tasks even when we do not feel like doing so. Discipline also requires listening to wise counsel when another way seems more attractive. In all your endeavours, seek counsel and train your ears to listen and heed advice. According to Jimi Hendrix, "Knowledge speaks but wisdom listens." Be also careful to manage your time your time well. This will keep you focused on the things that are important. There are 24 hours or 1440 minutes in each day. Carve out a specific time each day and focus on what needs to be done. Planning is fundamental in pursuing a discipline life. This includes managing your health, emotions, career, finances, and relationships. A disciplined approach is paramount to living a successful life.

Rules of the Game

4. **Mentorship** - Mentorship is critical for success. A mentor is usually someone who is more experienced in the target area. This person will therefore be able to provide advice and guidance as you navigate different aspects of life. We are never too old to have a mentor. Identify someone who has the traits that you aspire towards and see how you can form a relationship with them. Some persons may be willing to have regular check-in sessions to keep abreast with your progress, while others you can study even if you do not have a direct relationship with them. Within the shared relationship, mentorship fosters accountability and vulnerability. It also helps to build confidence as it gives you a cheerleader in the stands in the game of life.

5. **Support** – There is an old adage that says, "No man is an island." This continues to be true even in a world where a lot of praise is given those who are "self-made." The fact is that no matter how hard we work on our own, some form of support is needed to help us achieve our goals in life. For some persons, familial support is central to their sense of self and ability to thrive in life. Here, family may not be just blood relations, but anyone who has that permanent lifetime bond with us. A strong familial relationship however it manifests, is a safe place for us to be ourselves. Here, we can share our frustrations, pain, disappointments and desires, plans and victories.

Find that safe place for you and channel the support that you get from it to help you succeed in life.

If you are a part of a spiritual community, that support can also be vital in helping you achieve sustained growth and good success. A spiritual community can be mutually beneficial as you share your time and talents and also benefit from others. This community therefore provides the assurance that the support that you sow in the lives of others will also be given to you when you need it. Within these communities, some persons also create or participate in prayer groups. These groups foster dependency on the Sovereign One and also vulnerability as people share the concerns on their hearts. This, in turn, promotes connection and a sense in solidarity and faith in fulfilling one's life goals. which fosters connection. Indeed, "they that believe in the Lord shall never be disappointed" (Romans 9:33, NIV).

6. **Courage and Humility**— It takes a lot of courage to embark on a project that is unfamiliar and also to stick with it when things do not go according to plan. It also takes a lot of courage to remain unflinching in one's beliefs when the possibility of an easier but unscrupulous way of life is being dangled in front of you. It also requires humility to admit that we do not know everything and to ask for help. Life sometimes also humble us when our plans fail publicly. Courage

and humility are therefore two traits that go hand-in-hand in the quest for success. Be careful then to stay true to your values. Have the courage to not compromise your convictions, even when you are the only person standing firm. It can be a lonely journey, but remain true and persistent when obstacles or failures come. There is no shame in your game. Every winner has the courage to get back up again after failure. Have a servant's heart and a willingness to serve. This heart of service will make you attractive to those who are in a position to propel you into your destiny.

7. **Consistency** – We are the sum of our habits. The things that we continuously are therefore indicative of the type of success that we have in life. We therefore need to firstly create good winning habits and stick to them. This can be difficult in the initial stages when we do not see the results that we want. A plant, however, does not grow overnight. The gardener must be patient with the seed, watering it and giving it the right amounts of sunlight. You too must be steadfast as you repeatedly do the things that are vital. Do not compare yourself with others who seem to be achieving their goals much quicker than you. Be patient with yourself and the relationships that you are trying to cultivate. Stay in your lane, run your own race and stick to the plan.

8. **Work**—There are no shortcuts; you must do the work. Whether it is a forty-hour week or training,

work must be done. Usain Bolt, the Jamaican sprinter who has the men's 100 and 200 m world record once stated, *"For me, I am focused on what I want to do. I know what I need to do to be a champion, so I am working on it."* His name is forever etched in the annals of history because he did the work necessary to achieve world and Olympic glory. Through work, your skills will be sharpened, desires fulfilled, and visions actualised. There is also joy and satisfaction that result from seeing the rewards of your hard work. Your confidence will also soar and your belief in what is possible increased. Keep checking your scorecard as you work and learn lessons from your mistakes. Like Winston Churchill, believe that *"History will be kind to you as you are determined to write it."* Write the story of your life with hard work.

9. **Authenticity & Professionalism** - It is liberating for one to remain true to self and moral convictions. There is a freedom that comes from living from the script that you have for your life and not by deviating from it in order to please others. It is also refreshing for persons to engage with an authentic person; one feels connected to the simplicity of the humanness, vulnerability and honesty of character. Remaining authentic is one of the most beautiful contributions that we can give to life as we show others who we really are and invite them to be their true selves. This promotes connection as we do it life together. While being authentic, we should also strive to be

professional. This requires emotional intelligence, empathy and self-control. As authentic people, we can be honest and loyal, but when coupled with professionalism, we strive to respectful, trustworthy and humble. Knowing when, how, where and what to speak is the balance that the combination of authenticity and professionalism promotes. Be the best version of yourself as you authentically interact with others. Adorn yourself as well with professionalism. Professionalism is a brand. Wear it well.

10. **Keep Reinventing Yourself** — We live in an increasingly globalized world where innovations continue to change how we do business, interact and connect with others. This means that if we are not careful, our skills, knowledge and techniques can become outdated. If this happens, we may find ourselves losing in the game because our strategies are no longer applicable to the context in which we operate. To win the game, you must therefore stay current. Update your skills regularly. Take those professional development courses. Learn a new language. Attend those seminars in your field. Read journals and reports about the new technologies that are available and implement them in your work. Do not be afraid to think outside the box as you take on new initiatives. Your game strategies must change if you are to keep winning. To do this, you must be adaptable to change and keep reinventing yourself.

Game Over!

No game lasts forever. Every game has an allotted time and when that time expires, the game ends. Sometimes there is a tie and extra time is added to distinguish the winning team from the losing team. Depending on the game, penalties or sudden death where the next team that scores wins, may be used to end the game. All players, however, continue to play until the referee or umpire blows that final whistle signalling that the game is over.

In competitive games, the final whistle means the end of the game for all players. In life, however, we exit the game at different times. We know that we will have an exit, but we do not know when God, "Life's Umpire" will blow the final whistle on our time on earth. Until that whistle blows, we are therefore in the game and are expected to play by making the best use of our gifts and abilities. As you come to the close of this book, I therefore invite you to think about where you will spend eternity. What will be your destiny after you have batted your last innings on earth? If you have not yet done so, please take a moment to invite Jesus into your life. It makes no sense to win in this life but lose in the one to come. Make sure as you chart your many wins, get trophies, promotions and other accolades, that your scorecard is also positioning you to inherit a crown of life. Finally, live your life according to the real "Book of Rules" so that at the end you will hear your Maker say, "Well *done*, good and faithful servant; you have been faithful over a few things, I will make you ruler over many things. Enter into the joy of your Lord" (Matthew 25:23, NKJV). In this way, you will win in the game of life and also the one in eternity and importantly, it will be well with your soul.

BIBLIOGRAPHY

Forbes Profile. 2024. "Elon Musk." https://www.forbes.com/profile/elon-musk/ Accessed 1 July 2024.

GSMARena. 2015. "It All Began with a Failed Rice Cooker – A Glimpse at Sony's History." https://www.gsmarena.com/it_all_began_with_a_failed_rice_cooker_a_glimpse_at_sonys_history-blog-13661.php Accessed 1 July 2024.

International Olympic Committee. 2024. "The Olympic Symbol and Other Elements of the Olympic Identity." https://olympics.com/ioc/faq/olympic-symbol-and-identity/what-is-the-olympic-motto Accessed 2 July 2024.

Leadership and Sport. 2021. "What are the Different Types of Sports?" https://www.leadershipandsport.com/types-of-sports/ Accessed 2 July 2024.

Logan, Kristen. 2022. "Failure: Friend or Foe?" IBX Insights. https://insights.ibx.com/failure-friend-or-foe/ Accessed 1 July 2024.

Martin, David Sean. 2024. "The World's Celebrity Billionaires 2024." Forbes. https://www.forbes.com/sites/devinseanmartin/2024/04/02/the-worlds-celebrity-billionaires-2024-taylor-swift-kim-kardashian-oprah/ Accessed 1 July 2024.

MasterClass. 2021. "Basketball Rules Explained: Inside 16 Common Rules." https://www.masterclass.com/articles/basketball-rules-explained Accessed 2 July 2024.

Penn Museum. 2023. "The Games." https://www.penn.museum/sites/olympics/olympicorigins.shtml Accessed 2 July 2024.

Sakavitsi, Kalliopi. 2024. "The History of the Olympic Games." https://olympics.com/en/news/the-history-of-the-olympic-games Accessed 2 July 2024.

Simpson, George. 2020. "Elvis Presley: The Moment The King Got So Mad He Ripped His Shirt Off and Tore It in Two." https://www.express.co.uk/entertainment/music/1282748/Elvis-Presley-ripped-shirt-Jim-Denny-Grand-Ole-Opry-Ryman-Auditorium Accessed 1 July 2024.

Soccer.com. 2022. "The Basic Rules of Soccer: A Complete Guide." https://www.soccer.com/guide/rules-of-soccer-guide Accessed 2 July 2024.

The Kennedy Center. 2024. "Oprah Winfrey." https://www.kennedy-center.org/artists/w/wa-wn/oprah-winfrey/ Accessed 1 July 2024.

Wealthpreneur. 2023. "From Bankruptcy to Billionaire: Elon Musk's Inspirational Journey and Lessons for Equity Investors!" https://www.linkedin.com/pulse/from-bankruptcy-billionaire-elon-musks-inspirational-vinayak-vzmtc/ Accessed 1 July 2024.

Weltman, Barbara. 2021. "Lincoln's Lessons on Failure." https://bigideasforsmallbusiness.com/lincolns-lessons-on-failure/ Accessed 1 July 2024.

Yardley, William. 2013. "Eddie Bond, 79; Told Elvis He'd Never Make It a Singer." The Boston Globe. https://www.bostonglobe.com/metro/obituaries/2013/03/25/eddie-bond-rockabilly-singer-who-turned-down-elvis-presley-dies/xQxwPXrM1HY3uc2GbNgxxO/story.html Accessed 1 July 2024.

ABOUT THE AUTHOR

Susan is a sales executive, entrepreneur, social worker, sports enthusiast and philanthropist. Her passion for helping others reach their full potential is evident in her dedication to both her professional and volunteer work. She has over two decades of experience in the corporate world where she has served across industries and at different levels of leadership.

Susan's speaking engagements have brought her message to a wide audience, helping individuals and organizations reach their goals and achieve success. Susan Gordon

Kinnane is a true leader in every sense of the word. Her commitment to helping others, strong work ethic, and ability to inspire and motivate make her an asset to any team or organization. She continues to make a positive impact in her community and beyond, and her influence will undoubtedly continue to be felt for years to come.